Business Writing Skills

By Joseph Dobrian

Business Writing Skills/Joseph Dobrian

ISBN 0-8144-6410-6

First printing.

Table of Contents

CHAPTER 1

Getting Started

Why Write?

Many people say, "I hate to write!" But writing good, readable English is really not very hard. Still, many of us have convinced ourselves, somehow, that it is. (The cheerless way in which English is taught in many schools probably has a lot to do with our attitude!) Also, many people believe that as our society becomes more casual, the need for good writing skills will diminish. Good grammar and proper usage, to some people, have become something like good manners: stuffy formality that nobody cares about these days.

If you take that attitude, though, you're not going to make it in the business world, whether you're a manager or an administrative assistant. Aside from actually behaving badly, there is hardly anything that will hurt your reputation more surely than a poorly written letter or memo.

Think of the letters, memos and other communications you've received that were badly written. I'll bet that each one of them caused one of the following reactions:

> "I wish I could figure out what this person is saying."

> "I'm certainly not going to do business with anyone who hasn't bothered to learn to write well."

> "If she can't express herself any better than this on paper, imagine how she must sound in person!"

> "Don't they care enough to write decent letters?"

That last one is the cruncher. Writing in an interesting style, using clear, standard English, will tell your reader that you care about the reaction you're going to get. Not doing so implies that you don't care.

THE ONE BIG RULE OF GOOD WRITING

When you get right down to it, there's only one rule of good writing. The other "rules" aren't really rules at all. They are guidelines that help you to follow what I call the "One Big Rule," which is:

Brevity, precision and clarity—and the greatest of these is clarity.

We'll be coming back to the One Big Rule again and again in this book, as we cover punctuation, grammar, the use of foreign terms, the Fog Index, and the writing of effective letters, memos and reports. Keep it in mind as you go through the book, and keep it in mind, from now on, each time you write anything.

WHY WRITE WELL?

Now that you know the One Big Rule of good writing—which makes the whole process a lot less scary, doesn't it?—it's time to consider a few reasons for good writing:

- **Good writing makes you look good.** It gets you noticed, and it gets you promoted. It also gets you published. If you can write well, you can write articles in magazines, technical journals and newsletters—and having published an article on a certain subject makes you, officially, an expert on that subject.

- **Good writing makes your boss and your company look good.** If every communication that comes out of the office follows the One Big Rule, your boss will look good, the company will look good—and you'll get the credit.

- **It's an up and coming skill—believe it or not!** It seems that we have to document whatever we do in the office nowadays, whether it involves building a dossier on an employee so you can fire her later or charting your relationship with a supplier, or expanding your training manual. Writing of this sort must really be clear and precise! E–mail and other online services are becoming more widespread, and in many cases they're taking the place of phone conversations and face–to–face meetings. All in all, you'll be writing more, not less, as time goes on. Finally, English has become the international language of business. More and more people are writing it, all over the world. To communicate with all these people, you have to have good writing skills.

Anyone can learn to be a good writer. It's like any other skill: To get good at it, you have to want to be good at it, and you have to practice a lot. Write as much and as often as you can. Keep a diary; write letters to friends; write poetry, fiction and essays. Reading is just as important as writing. It doesn't much matter what you read so long as you read well–written books on the subjects that interest you. By reading good writing, you'll pick up all kinds of little tricks for making your own writing more interesting. You'll also expand your vocabulary and your understanding of the language.

The Blank Page (or Screen)

"Blank page syndrome" is that sinking feeling that you get when you sit down in front of the computer knowing that you have to write a letter, report or some other business document—and you don't have the first idea of how to start! You just sit there, feeling that you're the stupidest thing that ever drew breath. Finally, you remind yourself that if you don't write something, you won't get to go home, so you say what you have to say in the greatest possible number of words, in the hope that all those words will convince your reader that you know what you're talking about.

It's "blank-page syndrome" that makes a lot of people so afraid of writing. Just keep two things in mind, though. First, everyone suffers from it. Even Shakespeare probably had it sometimes. Second, it's easy to overcome, no matter how hopeless you're feeling.

The surest way to beat blank-page syndrome is not to begin at the beginning.

If you start your letter or report with an introductory passage, you'll sit there staring at the screen all day.

The first paragraphs should usually be the last thing you write. (It's a lot easier, nowadays, to write the beginning last, since you're likely to be working with a computer or word processor that lets you cut and paste blocks of copy as you work.) Where and how should you start, if not at the beginning? Every writer has an idea about that. How you get started depends a lot on how clear an idea you already have of what you want to say, how complicated the job is, and how thoroughly you understand the issue you're writing about. I have four methods, each of which has been very effective in different circumstances:

- **Start in the middle.** Just write. Start anywhere, but write down as much as you can write. If you have a sentence or paragraph in your mind, but you're not sure where it should go in the document, write it anyway, and work around it.

  If you're really stumped for something to say, start by writing down whatever you know about the issue you're addressing. Suppose, for instance, that you're writing a brief report on a conference you attended. You remember what you did at the conference, so start by stating the plain facts: "On Monday morning I attended the general session, where the keynote speaker was...." From that, you'll get into a description of the main points of the speech. Following that, you'll describe the seminars you attended, the exhibits you saw, and so on. Before you know it, you'll have written a major portion of your report.

  Now that you've done the purely descriptive writing, go over the document and identify the most important points. For example, maybe a new product was introduced at this conference, a product that you think will revolutionize your industry. In that case, it's that new product, more than the conference, that you'll want to focus on. You then can write the beginning of the report:

  > "The highlight of last week's Gadgets Unlimited Conference was the introduction of a left-handed hoozenhaffer which is likely to cut our labor costs by about 40 percent within the next two years."

- **Write an informal outline.** Nobody enjoys writing outlines: They're not interesting, and we usually end up ignoring them anyway. But sometimes they do help. You don't have to write a fancy one, with lots of Roman numerals and sub-headings. Just jot down the points you want to cover, then figure out which points are the most important and—very generally—what you want to say about each. Keep on jotting down ideas, jumping from point to point as you think of something else to say.

  Before too long, you'll have written most of what you need to write. Now it's just a matter of putting those ideas into complete sentences and putting the ideas into their proper order. When that's done, you'll be ready to write your introduction and your conclusion.

- **Work backwards.** If you already know what your conclusion is going to be, but don't know how you're going to bring the reader to it, start by writing the conclusion:

"Therefore, all rules against smoking should be abolished."

You have just written your whole story in one sentence. All you have to do now is supply the "why" and the "how." Just write your reasons for wanting the anti-smoking rules abolished, as they come to you. Later, you can worry about putting them in the right order. For now, just get them onto the screen, along with whatever arguments or evidence you might have to back them up.

You've now written the middle and the end of the document. Now it should be easy to determine the beginning, something like, "Doctors at the North Carolina Research Center have concluded that, contrary to popular belief, smoking is good for you!"

- **Ask, "Why am I doing this?"** One good way to get your motor running is to start before the beginning. In other words, write an explanation (to yourself) of why you have to write this document. For instance: "I need to write a letter to the Mayor's office applying for permission to build an addition to our factory despite city zoning codes. The problem is that the land we want to build on is zoned as a street. Even though it's actually just a big field of gravel—so, technically, we'd be building in the middle of the street!" Before you know it, you'll have written most of the information that will have to go into the letter. Now it's just a matter of reorganizing and editing that material into a clearer, more concise form:

> Dear Mayor Dale:
>
> I am writing this letter to request an exemption from Rule 6.12 of the Montgomery zoning code.
>
> Our firm intends to build an addition on lot 5683, which the Zoning Commission has zoned as a street. However, as the enclosed photographs show, this lot is actually a field of gravel.

There you are: You're rolling!

Writing to Your Audience

Naturally, you will use different tones depending on what you're writing and whom you're addressing. A letter of complaint will usually be crisp and businesslike; an annual report will be rather formal but upbeat; a sales brochure might be dynamic, almost breathless. Your letters and memos will sometimes be friendly and chatty, sometimes formal and impersonal. But in each case, you will follow the One Big Rule:

Brevity, precision and clarity—and the greatest of these is clarity.

Some experts believe that the best way to adjust the tone of your writing is to write the way you speak. In other words, if you were writing one letter to your mother and another to a corporate president, you would write each letter as though you were talking to the person in question. This advice is good but is often misunderstood. The tone has much more to do with your personal relationship with the recipient than with his or her social position.

A good way to restate that advice is: The friendlier you are with your audience, the more informal and idiomatic you can be. (For instance, if you were very friendly with the corporate president, there'd be no objection to your writing, "Dear Sam, Guess what? I broke 80 yesterday! Nice shootin', huh? By the way, I wonder if you could tell me....")

Notice I said, "The friendlier you are," and not "the friendlier you're trying to be." Never take a chummy tone with people you don't know in an effort to show them how folksy and likable you are. Such a tone might not actually offend them, but it will make them think you're insincere.

Spoken English is much easier with the rules than written English. Probably nobody in the world speaks perfectly standard English. We'll use "got" and "gotten" interchangeably; we'll say, "The man that I was speaking with," or "it's a couple of miles further on," and nobody will hold it against us. When you write, your reader will expect you to avoid such mistakes—whatever your relationship.

This doesn't mean that you should be excessively formal in your writing. Nobody likes to read something like, "It is to be hoped that within the next 30-day period you will have given consideration to my proposals and will be prepared to deliver a detailed response." If you were speaking this idea, rather than writing it, you'd say it in one of several ways:

Very informal:

Get back to me on this in a month or so, okay?

Informal:

Could you please get back to me on these proposals within a month's time?

Formal:

I hope you'll be able to respond to these proposals no later than a month from now.

Each of those three sentences is clear, concise and brief, and each works just as well written as it does spoken.

Probably the best way to adjust your writing for your audience is just to state the information you're trying to communicate, with no trimming of any kind. Having done that, you can make whatever adjustments you feel are necessary.

For example, suppose you're writing a memo to a colleague, informing her that you want to meet with her. Start by writing:

I want to see you about ABC at three o'clock tomorrow afternoon.

Now, rewrite the sentence, depending on how you want to sound:

Friendly, easy-going:

I need to see you about ABC. Could you come by my office at three tomorrow?

Forceful, impersonal:

We will discuss ABC in my office at three o'clock tomorrow.

Extremely informal:

About ABC: My office, tomorrow at three?

Formal, respectful:

If it's convenient for you, I'd like to discuss ABC in my office at three o'clock tomorrow.

Terminology

Before we go any further, let's discuss very briefly the parts of speech. The list below is not an exhaustive lesson in English grammar. It's just meant to help you understand the terminology, in case you're not clear on some of the definitions.

A really thorough study of English grammar is a huge project—but believe it or not, it can be fun. Oddly enough, the best way to learn English grammar is to learn another language—particularly French or Latin—then study English more intensely.

Types of Words

NOUNS

A noun is a word (or a compound word) that names something. *Dog, father, water* and *sky* are nouns; *son-in-law* is a compound noun.

PROPER NOUNS

Proper nouns are names of specific persons or things. *Henry, Argentina, Mrs. Robinson* and *Jeep Cherokee* are all proper nouns. Proper nouns are almost always capitalized.

PRONOUNS

Pronouns take the place of nouns, proper nouns and noun equivalents. *I, he, they, me* and *him* are personal pronouns, and refer to specific persons:

> I spoke with Mr. Seaforth. He's smarter than he looks.

Indefinite pronouns do not refer to specific people or things. *Everybody, each, one,* and *something* are indefinite pronouns:

> One sometimes forgets that nobody likes a whiner.

Demonstrative pronouns include words like *this* and *that*:

> This is the best hamburger I've ever tasted!

Words like *that, which, who* and *whom* are relative pronouns and introduce subordinate clauses or phrases:

>The office manager will issue passes to employees
>who need to enter the building on weekends.

In other contexts, words like *who* and *which* are interrogative pronouns:

>Who told you that?

Words like *himself* and *yourself* are reflexive pronouns, because they reflect onto the subject of the sentence:

>He washed himself.

ADJECTIVE

Adjectives describe or modify a noun. *Thin, perfect,* and *yellow* are adjectives. Some adjectives are comparative—that is, they indicate a greater degree than the thing to which the noun is being compared:

>Most people think Curly was funnier than Shemp.

Some are superlative—indicating the greatest degree of a certain quality:

>James I was nicknamed "The Wisest Fool in Christendom."

ADVERB

Adverbs usually modify verbs or adjectives, but they can also modify other adverbs, prepositions, and whole phrases, clauses and sentences. Many adverbs are adjectives with *ly* tacked onto them: *stupidly, aimlessly, philosophically.* Words like *now, also, very* and *indeed* are also adverbs.

VERB

A verb expresses an action. *Jump, read* and *eat* are verbs. A verb's spelling and pronunciation will change according to tense (past, present, progressive, future, etc.), mood (indicative, subjunctive, imperative) and voice (active or passive).

ARTICLE

The definite article is *the,* as in "the hat," which means "that particular hat." The indefinite article is *a* as in "a hat," which means "any hat." A becomes *an* when connected to a word that begins with a vowel or with a silent or unstressed *h*—for instance, "an eagle" or "an honorable gesture" but "*a* hero"!

PREPOSITION

Prepositions indicate place, direction or relation. *To, against, with* and *despite* are prepositions. *In reference to* and *by way of* are compound prepositions.

CONJUNCTION

Conjunctions are words that link two clauses, such as *as, but, for* and *since*. Many words serve as either conjunctions or prepositions, depending on their role in the sentence.

INTERJECTION

Interjections are sounds, single words, or phrases that do not, strictly speaking, constitute complete sentences. They may stand alone or as part of a sentence. Some examples:

> Ouch!

> Ha! I fooled you!

> Well, I'll try.

> My boss—the jerk!—made me come in on Saturday.

This is important! Remember that only some words are *only* nouns, only verbs, etc. Many words can be any of several types, depending on the context. In the sentence, "He told you a lie," the word *lie* is a noun. But in the sentence, "I lie all the time," it's a verb!

Putting Words Together

PHRASE

A phrase consists of two or more words that are related to each other, but which do not form a complete sentence. In spoken English, a phrase often acts as a complete sentence:

> Not at all.

> Absolutely not!

In written English, however, a phrase must almost always be part of a complete sentence.

CLAUSE

A clause contains a subject (or a subject phrase) and a predicate phrase. A subject refers to the person or thing that is the subject of the sentence; the predicate phrase contains the verb and any adjectives or adverbs. Some clauses may also be expressed as complete sentences.

> He is a man whose head is in the clouds.

This sentence has two clauses: "He is a man" and "head is in the clouds." ("Whose" is a relative pronoun that links the clauses.) In the first clause, "He" is the subject; "is a man" is the predicate. In the second clause, "head" is the subject; "is in the clouds" is the predicate.

SENTENCE

A sentence can express a statement, a question, a command or an exclamation. One example of each will do:

> I'm the smartest, most talented person in the office.

> Don't you think I'm the humblest person in the world?

> Tell me the truth!

> Holy Toledo!

With the exception of exclamations, a complete sentence must have at least one complete clause—that is, a subject and a predicate. A simple sentence has one subject and one predicate:

> I write.

A compound sentence has two or more main clauses—that is, clauses of equal importance:

> You could remain a Democrat, or you could join the Republicans.

A complex sentence has a main clause and one or more clauses that are dependent on the main clause:

> He hit me so hard that I staggered and fell.

Writing sentences that are both easy to read and stylistically beautiful takes a lot of practice. The best way to learn how to do this is to read the works of great essayists and novelists from the 18th century to the present, and try to hear the music that their words produce.

Of course, when you're writing for business, you're not trying to be a great stylist. But you do want your writing to have an effect on people, and if you have a strong style, your writing will be very effective indeed.

PARAGRAPH

If two paragraphs do not clearly relate to each other, you should find a way to link them together. You can do this by suggesting at the end of one paragraph what you're going to talk about in the next one, or you can refer to an idea in the previous paragraph at the beginning of a new one. A third method of linkage is to insert a very short transitional paragraph:

> Now that I've gone on for so long about that sales meeting,
> I'd better say something about next year's budget.

You may have learned, once, that a paragraph must have at least two sentences. There is no such rule. It's true that it's usually a good idea to put several sentences into a paragraph: Too many one-sentence paragraphs will make your writing look very choppy. However, the occasional one-sentence paragraph will give your writing variety and emphasis.

So there.

EXERCISES

I. In the following sentences, identify the type of each word (noun, verb, adjective, etc.):

1. **My cat is completely black.**
2. **Everything that I say is a lie.**
3. **I work for a company called Dobrian, Logart & Frances.**
4. **What are you talking about?**

II. In those same four sentences, identify subjects and predicates. (The fourth sentence is very tricky. Don't feel bad if you don't get it. I explain it at the back of the book on page 113.)

CHAPTER 2

The Style Book

"Correct" English

There is no such thing as "correct" English.

That sounds crazy, but if you think about it for a moment, you'll find that it's the truth. Your pronunciation, grammar and vocabulary are different from the Queen of England's, from Madonna's, and from Jesse Jackson's—and who's to say which of the four of you is using correct English?

Some language experts talk about "standard English" and "substandard English," but each expert seems to have a different idea of what "standard" means. In any case, standards change all the time.

About the time the Pilgrims were landing in America, "I didn't do nothing" was considered standard. George Washington would have said (or written), "I eat a whole chicken last night," instead of "I ate," and he would have pronounced the word "et." English–speakers of Abraham Lincoln's time would have said, "It don't matter." There are still many people who believe there's nothing wrong with saying, "I ain't going."

If you listen, you'll notice language evolving every day. For example, have you noticed lately how many teenage girls, instead of saying, "He said, 'I can't go out tonight,'" will say, "He's like, "I can't go out tonight"? That expression is considered substandard English today, but in a generation or so, "He's like" might be a standard way of saying "He said." Who knows?

Why are there so many different ways of expressing yourself in English? And why does the language continue to change so much? Probably the best answer to both of those questions is that English is really a hodgepodge of lots of other languages. Therefore, nobody has ever been able to come up with a set of iron–clad rules regarding spelling, grammar, punctuation and usage.

(In France, about 350 years ago a group of scholars formed an organization called the Académie Française to standardize the rules of "correct"

French. As a result, French is a much more standardized language than English is—but even the Académie has to change its rules from time to time to allow for foreign words or variant spellings.)

As you probably know, English evolved in Britain. In very early times, the people of Britain spoke Celtic languages. (Modern Celtic languages include Gaelic, which is still spoken in parts of Ireland and Scotland; Welsh; and Breton, which is spoken in northwestern France. In Scotland, some people still speak a language called Scots, which sounds somewhat like English but contains many Gaelic words, constructions and pronunciations. Things change, though, and Scots is now a dying language.)

The Romans conquered Britain in the first century A. D. , and since they made Latin the official language of government, many Latin words and grammatical rules found their way into general use.

In the fifth century, as the Roman Empire collapsed, Britain was overrun by the Saxons, a Germanic tribe that spoke an early form of German. Later, the Vikings conquered much of England and Scotland and introduced their own language, an early form of Danish. (The Viking language survives today in Iceland, still spoken pretty much as it was 1,000 years ago, since nobody else ever invaded Iceland.)

In 1066, Duke William of Normandy (which is part of France) invaded England and claimed the English throne. Naturally, he rewarded his friends and allies with land and titles in England—and the result was that French quickly became the language of the upper classes. The kings and queens of England spoke French as their everyday language for the next 300 years or so—some of them couldn't speak English at all!

That, by the way, is why we say "cow" to describe the animal in the field, but "beef" to refer to the meat on the table: The farmers who raised the animal used the Anglo-Saxon word *cu*—but the upper-class landowners who ate the animal used the French word *boeuf*.

At any rate, English gradually started to sound something like the language we speak today—but as you might imagine, it grew in different ways in different places, as it still does. American and British people pronounce the language differently, but the main difference between American and British English is that American English has adopted a great many more foreign words, mainly from German, Spanish and various West African languages.

To this day, English-speakers have many different ideas of how the language should sound. (For instance, a "Teuchter" from the Scottish Highlands and a "Cajun" from southern Louisiana would hardly understand each other at all.)

As diverse as spoken English may be, though, written English comes pretty close to being the same wherever you go. That Scotsman and his friend from Louisiana would have no problem reading each other's letters!

In this chapter, we'll cover English grammar, punctuation, usage and spelling as applied to written English.

What Is a Style Book?

A style book tells you what is "correct" English for your purposes. A style book says, in effect, "Okay, we all have our own opinions on what's right and what's not, and we all have our own rules. Well, these are the rules for anything you write in this office."

Some companies, such as newspaper and magazine publishers, have enormous style books that cover everything. Other companies have smaller, less formal style books. The style book that follows here is not complete, but it will give you enough information to let you write well.

If you want a more complete style book, *The Chicago Manual of Style* is considered to be a good one; so is the *Associated Press Style Book*. You will find, however, that no two style books agree on everything. Each of the books cited here will disagree with this book on some points. But all of these books, in their different ways, give you standard rules.

Punctuation

APOSTROPHE

The apostrophe is used to indicate missing letters (*didn't*) or a possessive (*Bill's*). Do not use an apostrophe to form a plural (I like hot dogs). Do not use an apostrophe when speaking of a family. ("The Smiths" is the proper way to refer to the Smith family. "The Smith's" would mean either "The Smith is" or "something that belongs to The Smith.")

Form the possessive of a noun or proper noun by adding 's (the dog's bone; Anne's house). Use only an apostrophe when forming the possessive of a plural noun ending in s (the dogs' bones; farmers' market). Proper nouns of two or more syllables ending in s or z become possessive with only an apostrophe (Velazquez' paintings).

BRACKETS

Use brackets to set off information that you are inserting into a direct quote. This information could include corrections, explanations, elaborations and missing words or letters. Bracketed information may also appear immediately after the direct quote. Here are some examples:

> "I'm only 39 [Born in 1946, she is actually 49.], and
> I'm already a grandmother!"

> "I was talking with Rocky Marciano [the former Heavyweight
> Champion of the World] when my future wife entered the room."

> "We've got to keep this information away from N[ixon]."

COLON

Use a colon to introduce:

- A sentence, phrase or word that relates closely to whatever came before the colon:

> She's an attractive woman: Her eyes are especially beautiful.

- A particularly important phrase:

> Don't forget: She's not easy to fool.

- A list:

> There were four Beatles: Paul, George, John and Ringo.

- A quote that's being given special emphasis:

> It's in the Bible: "Thou shalt not steal."

- A colon also punctuates the salutation of a business letter:

> Dear Sir:

COMMA

Since the comma is the most used punctuation mark in English, it's often overused. Its main uses are to indicate a slight pause between parts of a sentence and to introduce new ideas within a sentence.

Here are a few examples of how to use a comma in business writing:

> I didn't show up on time, so he thought I was careless.

Here, the comma connects two thoughts: "I didn't show up on time," and "He thought I was careless." The comma indicates that "He thought I was careless" was a consequence of "I didn't show up on time."

> My boss, Ms. O'Reilly, can speak Swahili.

In the sentence above, the commas set off the phrase "Ms. O'Reilly," which specifies the phrase "my boss."

In the next sentence, the commas separate a parenthetical phrase from the rest of the sentence. The phrase is parenthetical because it is not critical to identifying the job steward. If there were several shop stewards, then the information about this steward would be critical, and the commas would be removed.

> Our shop steward, who is deaf, is teaching us sign language.

In the sentence below, the commas separate items in a list. Some style books suggest that a comma appear before the word *and*. We prefer to leave out the comma before the *and*.

> I had bacon, eggs, toast, juice and coffee.

Use a comma to set off a direct address:

> Ms. Johnson, I don't think we should do this.

A comma can also be used following a mild interjection:

> Oh, he's the stupidest man you'd ever want to meet.

It can also be used to separate two or more adjectives:

> He's an honest, hard-working employee.

Use a comma to introduce a direct quotation:

> Jim said, "I'm going to ask for a raise."

Commas separate a quotation from the phrase that identifies the speaker.

> "I'm going to China," she cried, "and I'm not coming back!"

Always use a comma after a date:

> In 1947, the British granted independence to India.

Commas can take the place of words that would otherwise have to be repeated. Here, the comma between "some" and "when" implies the words "kill their love."

> Some kill their love when they are young, and some,
> when they are old.

Use a comma following the salutation of an informal letter, and following the complimentary close of a formal or an informal letter:

> Dear Ed, . . . Sincerely,

Insert a comma between a proper name and an affiliation, degree or title:

> William B. Jones, Ph. D.

Do not use a comma next to any other punctuation mark that indicates a pause or an interjection, such as brackets, colons, dashes, ellipsis, parentheses or semicolons, or with any mark indicating a full stop, such as exclamation points, periods and question marks.

Commas should also not be used to separate verbs:

> He kissed me and told me he'd be back.

But do use commas to indicate a series of actions:

> He kissed me, punched my brother in the nose, and told me he'd be back.

Commas shouldn't be used to introduce an indirect quotation:

> He said he was thinking of quitting.

In many cases, commas should be used simply because a sentence looks better with them than without them. For instance, anyone can understand the sentences below:

> I was an intelligent if mischievous little boy.

> It's you not I who's going to get into trouble.

These sentences are easier to read, though, if you use commas to set off the qualifying phrases:

> I was an intelligent, if mischievous, little boy.

> It's you, not I, who's going to get into trouble.

Sometimes, you'll use a comma to indicate the speed with which a sentence should be read. Consider this sentence:

> I never liked you and I never will.

Now add a comma:

> I never liked you, and I never will.

With a comma, the sentence reads more slowly and is more emphatic.

DASH

You may use a dash to set off an explanation or elaboration, in place of a colon:

> She never takes no for an answer—that's why she makes so many sales.

It's also a less formal, but punchier, equivalent to parentheses:

> My husband—who is very clumsy in most ways—is a pretty good dancer.

A dash can be used as a stronger version of a comma:

> He can barely speak English—which is a big problem.

A dash can also indicate surprise or irony:

> My boss just signed a three-year contract—with our main competitor!

Dashes are useful if you're combining two or more parenthetical phrases. Use a dash for the more important parenthetical phrase and parentheses for the less important:

> We've notified all our biggest clients—Andy, Stanley, Aunt Bea, and Herman (Stanley's cousin).

You may use dashes with exclamation points and question marks:

> By the time the speaker sat down, I was—and who wasn't?—ready to fall asleep.

Do not use a dash to introduce a list. Use a colon instead:

> You need four things to succeed as a boxer: strength, stamina, intelligence and determination.

ELLIPSIS

 These three dots, so widely used in diaries and love-letters, have almost no place in business writing. Probably the only time you'll use them is to indicate some missing words in a direct quote:

> His report. . . was full of mistakes.

Never use ellipsis to indicate a break in the structure of a sentence or to set off an interjected phrase.

EXCLAMATION POINT

 Use an exclamation point to express emphasis or strong emotion. (Don't use it frequently in your writing, however, as overuse will reduce its impact.) You may use an exclamation point at the end of a sentence, like a period, or between two dashes:

> That was the worst foul-up I've ever seen!

> My former employers—the cheapskates!—only gave me
> one raise in five years.

HYPHEN

 Use hyphens to link elements in compound words if the compound is not regarded as a word in itself—as in "one-man dog."

In most cases, compound words don't require hyphens. For instance, "ice cream" is such a common compound noun that it doesn't need a hyphen. "Whitewalls" are now so well known that the term has become one word (as opposed to "white walls," which have nothing to do with tires). Even compounds like "airhead" have become so generally known that they've become words in themselves.

Avoid long hyphenated phrases such as the one in this sentence: "He won the worst–dressed–golfer–on–the–course award." Say instead, "He won the award for being the worst–dressed golfer on the course. " (You can't say, "worst dressed golfer," without the hyphen, because that might imply that he was the worst of the golfers who were dressed—although there might have been a few nude golfers who were even worse!)

Don't use a hyphen to separate an adverb ending in *ly* and the following verb:

> "It was a cleverly crafted question. "

Use a hyphen between an adverb and a verb if the adverb does not end in *ly*: "That's a well-made suit." Drop the hyphen if you turn the phrase around: "The suit is well made."

Hyphenate combined adjectives if you would cause confusion by not hyphenating them: "Black-and-white cats" means that each of the cats is black and white. "Black and white cats" implies that some of the cats are white, and some are black.

Do not hyphenate familiar compound nouns used as adjectives, such as "real estate office." But hyphenate unusual compound nouns used as adjectives if you feel that their meaning might otherwise be misunderstood, such as "striped-pants boys."

Use hyphens to connect a prefix with the word to be modified if the prefix is not a word in itself, as in "pre-war foreign policy." Use a hyphen if a prefix that is not a word is standing alone, as in "pre- and post-war foreign policies."

PARENTHESES

Parentheses are used much like dashes, to set off a sentence or phrase that supplements the main sentence:

> Only two original members of Steely Dan (Donald Fagen and Walter Becker) were still with the band when "Gaucho" was recorded.

> Mangas Coloradas was "shot while trying to escape" (that is, murdered by his guards), as were many Indian chiefs who resisted the whites.

Use parentheses to provide cross-references:

> We must revise our sales goals for the coming year (see my last letter).

> The map of Cincinnati (p. 246) will show you how I plan to rezone the city.

Or to enclose supplementary quotations:

> He made several cynical remarks ("All bosses are liars"; "All vice-presidents are nobodies"), which annoyed me.

As you see, material between parentheses does not end with a period unless it stands completely outside any other sentence:

> Yesterday, I ran into a former colleague. (Naturally, I pretended that I was happy to see her.)

In this sentence, you'll observe, the parentheses aren't really necessary, but they serve to give the last sentence a confidential air: It's as though the writer is giving you a nudge and a wink.

PERIOD

A period indicates the end of a sentence and punctuates some abbreviations. (For more on the use of the period in abbreviations, see page 34.) Use a period after someone's initials (G. A. Brown) unless the person is known by his intitals (JFK, FDR).

QUESTION MARK

A question mark is used at the end of a direct question, but it doesn't have to come at the end of a sentence.

> Will you take tea or coffee?

> Did she resign? was the question we all wanted to ask.

> Are you a secretary? an executive assistant? an administrative assistant?

A question mark in parentheses indicates uncertainty:

> I once met Lee Harvey Oswald, the murderer (?) of President Kennedy.

QUOTATION MARKS

Use double quotation marks (also called "double quotes"):

• On either side of a direct quotation:

> She said, "I'm going to be an opera star."

• Even if the quotation isn't a complete sentence:

> He said he would vote for you "when hell freezes over."

• Around words borrowed from others:

> As Jim would say, this guy is a real "go-getter."

- Around words that you're speaking of as words:

> There's no "but" in Butterfield!

- But not around individual letters:

> He got an A in English.

- Around translations of foreign proper nouns or slang terms—usually within parentheses:

> Powhatan named his daughter Pocahontas ("mischievous one").

> They presented us with a *fait accompli* (a "done deal").

- But not around translations of other foreign words or phrases:

> He was elected *taoiseach* (prime minister) of Ireland.

- To denote sarcasm:

> The boss signed us up to do "volunteer" work at the hospital.

- To set off a definition, for the sake of clarity:

> The word awful can mean "very unpleasant" or "remarkable. "

- But not around indirect quotes:

> She said something about having to leave early.

- Don't use double quotes around slang terms, either. It looks too self-conscious if you write something like,

> The presentation was "way cool."

If you feel that the rest of what you're writing is too formal to allow a slang expression, don't use it at all. If you feel that the expression may be used, it doesn't need quotation marks.

- Use single quotes to enclose a quotation within a quotation:

> I told her, "Don't call him 'Shorty' to his face!"

- Place commas and periods inside quotation marks:

> Her voice said, "yes," but her eyes said, "no."

- Colons and semicolons, on the other hand, always go outside quotation marks. For instance:

> He called me a "whiz kid": I think that means he likes my work.

- Question marks and exclamation points go inside the quotation mark if they are a part of the quotation, outside the quotation mark if they are part of a larger sentence:

    > "What do you think of my car?" he asked.

    but

    > Did you really call the boss "an autocrat"?

- If a quotation continues from one paragraph to another, do not use quotation marks at the end of a paragraph, but do use them to introduce the new paragraph. Close the quotation only at the very end:

    > "I'm an honest woman," she said. "Sure, I bet on football games, but I've never been involved in shaving points or fixing games.
    >
    > "I haven't even heard of that sort of thing more than once or twice in my life, and I've been betting on football ever since Teddy Roosevelt threatened to ban it."

SEMICOLON

A semicolon looks like a combination of a comma and a period, and that's just about what it is. It usually takes the place of a conjunction, to separate two related clauses of a sentence:

> Some people thought that the boss was really angry; I knew he was just kidding.

- Use a semicolon to separate two clauses if the second clause is elliptical (that is, if it leaves out one or more words that are implied from the first clause):

    > He's very tall; his wife, very short.

- Semicolons separate two clauses when the second begins with a conjunctive adverb or phrase, such as *consequently, still,* or *on the contrary:*

    > I speak French pretty well; therefore, I learned Creole quickly.

- Use semicolons instead of commas in a list of long items or items containing commas:

    > I fired him for several reasons: He was consistently late; he insulted my assistant; he smoked at his desk; he stole from petty cash; and he insisted that he had an "evil twin," named Skippy, who was doing all these things.

SLASH

A slash can represent small words such as *or, to, and* and *at:*

> Bed/dresser set

> his/her

> the New York/New Jersey/Connecticut metropolitan area

Slashes sometimes appear in abbreviations:

> d/b/a (doing business as)

> c/o (in care of)

> a/k/a (also known as)

Capitalization, Plurals, Possessives and Abbreviations

CAPITALIZATION

Capitalize:

- Proper names (John Anderson) and titles when they're used as part of a name (the Duke of Cumberland, President William Clinton; Her Majesty Queen Elizabeth II);

- Nicknames (Long John Silver; Old Hickory);

- Full names of businesses (American Express), organizations (Southern Christian Leadership Conference), cultural centers (Carnegie Hall), government agencies (the Central Intelligence Agency) and slang terms for such organizations (Ma Bell);

- Geographic terms, including slang terms (the Western Hemisphere, the Old West, the Mississippi River, the East Village, the Windy City);

- The first word of a complete sentence or a direct quotation;

- The first word of a sentence within a sentence, such as a proverb or a direct question (As I always say, He who laughs last doesn't get the joke.);

- The first word following a colon if the words following the colon form a complete sentence (I love Liszt's piano music: My favorite piece is his Sixth Hungarian Rhapsody);
- The first word of a salutation or close of a letter (Dear Ms. Lincoln: Yours truly,); the first letter of an abbreviation of a capitalized word (Mex.);
- Languages, nationalities, races and religions (French, Polynesian, Muslim);
- Laws and principles (Murphy's Law);
- Days of the week, months and holidays;
- Letters of the alphabet when you're referring to them as letters ("Fish" begins with an F);
- All words (except short articles, conjuctions and prepositions) in titles of books, plays, films and periodicals (*Pride and Prejudice*);
- Trademarks (Coca-Cola).

Do not capitalize:

- Titles when they're not part of a name (Roger Simmons, president of General Electric);
- The first word following a colon if the words following the colon do not form a complete sentence (I had my favorite dish for dinner: pork chops.);
- Seasons of the year;
- "Important" words ("I miss my dear wife, Dorothy," not "I miss my Dear Wife, Dorothy.").

PLURALS

English is full of "irregular plurals"—that is, plural forms that end with something other than s or es. Most of these, you know already—and you use them without noticing them. (Think of man/men; foot/feet; ox/oxen; mouse/mice.) A few, however, are tricky.

The regular rule is this: You form a plural by adding s to most words. To words ending in s, x, z, ch or sh, you usually have to add es. If the word ends with a y preceded by a consonant, change the y to an i and add es (baby/babies). If a word ends with f or fe, the plural usually ends in ves (life/lives; leaf/leaves).

Do not use 's to denote a plural. The sole exception is if you're pluralizing a lower-case letter of the alphabet. (Be sure to dot your i's and cross your t's.)

In many cases, you won't know that a certain word has an irregular plural. If you're in any doubt at all, you'll just have to look the word up in the dictionary. However, there are certain types of words that are likely to have irregular plurals.

- Many animal names have the same form in the singular and the plural (moose, quail, trout).

- Words derived from classical languages (Latin, Greek, Hebrew) often have irregular plurals (stadium/stadia; alumnus/alumni; index/indices; Hasid/Hasidim).

- Foreign terms should be pluralized in their original languages (beau/beaux or tempo/tempi). In most cases, a good English dictionary will supply the correct plural forms.

- Pluralize compound terms that consist of a noun and an adjective by adding s or es to the noun, not the adjective (attorney general/attorneys general; heir apparent/heirs apparent).

POSSESSIVES

To form the possessive case of most nouns or proper names, add 's.

If a noun ends in s or z, you might want to add only an apostrophe. This is a point on which nobody seems to agree. Some people feel that if a word would be easy to pronounce with an extra s (boss's, for instance), you should add 's; if the word would turn into a toungue-twister with an extra s (exterminators's), then the final s should be left off (exterminators'). Most people prefer to pluralize a proper name ending in s with only an apostrophe (Barnes'), although 's (Barnes's) is often acceptable.

It's this kind of thing that makes it advisable for an office to have its own style book. If you have your own house rules as to when to use 's and when not to, then you might still have some people thinking that you're not using good English, but at least you'll be able to defend yourself by saying, "It's just our style!"

ABBREVIATIONS

When should you use abbreviations?

Abbreviations should not be over-used in business writing. The best rule to follow is, "When in doubt, spell it out." There are, however, a good many words that may be abbreviated in business writing:

• Days of the week should not be abbreviated, but months other than May, June and July may be.

• States should be abbreviated only if they're part of an address: Use the old-fashioned abbreviations in letters and reports, but use the two-letter post-office abbreviations when addressing envelopes.

State	Old-Fashioned	Post Office
Alabama	Ala.	AL
Alaska	Alas.	AK
Arizona	Ariz.	AZ
Arkansas	Ark.	AR
California	Calif.	CA
Colorado	Colo.	CO
Connecticut	Conn.	CT
Delaware	Del.	DE
District of Columbia	D. C.	DC
Florida	Fla.	FL
Georgia	Ga.	GA
Hawaii	Hawaii	HI
Idaho	Ida.	ID
Illinois	Ill.	IL
Indiana	Ind.	IN
Iowa	Iowa	IA
Kansas	Kans.	KS
Kentucky	Ky.	KY
Louisiana	La.	LA
Maine	Me.	ME
Maryland	Md.	MD
Massachusetts	Mass.	MA
Michigan	Mich.	MI
Minnesota	Minn.	MN
Mississippi	Miss.	MS
Missouri	Mo.	MO
Montana	Mont.	MT
Nebraska	Nebr.	NE
Nevada	Nev.	NV

State	Old-Fashioned	Post Office
New Hampshire	N. H.	NH
New Jersey	N. J.	NJ
New Mexico	N. M.	NM
New York	N. Y.	NY
North Carolina	N. C.	NC
North Dakota	N. D.	ND
Ohio	Ohio	OH
Oklahoma	Okla.	OK
Oregon	Ore.	OR
Pennsylvania	Penn.	PA
Rhode Island	R. I.	RI
South Carolina	S. C.	SC
South Dakota	S. D.	SD
Tennessee	Tenn.	TN
Texas	Texas	TX
Utah	Utah	UT
Vermont	Vt.	VT
Virginia	Va.	VA
Washington	Wash.	WA
West Virginia	W. Va.	WV
Wisconsin	Wisc.	WI
Wyoming	Wyo.	WY

- Use abbreviations in street addresses: St., Ave., Rd. Abbreviate directions if they're part of an address, like "15th St. NW," but spell them out if you're describing a region or direction, such as "I'm walking northwest."

- Spell out the names of associations, schools, organizations and agencies on first reference, with the abbreviation in parentheses; then abbreviate all further references:

> The International Ladies' Garment Workers Union (ILGWU) has agreed to represent employees of Fruit of the Loom. An ILGWU spokesperson said she expected the union to have a good relationship with the company's management.

- Abbreviate commonly used words in company names, such as Corp., Inc. and Bros.

- Abbreviate titles and military ranks, such as Mrs., Dr., Col. and Rev.

- Don't abbreviate weights or measures unless they're part of a recipe.
- Don't ever begin a sentence with an abbreviation.

How do you punctuate abbreviations?

- When two or more words are abbreviated with their initial letters, use periods (as in I. Q.), unless the abbreviation is an acronym (an abbreviation that's spoken as a word), such as NATO, an organization, like the FBI, or a trade name, like PC. (You would use periods to abbreviate "politically correct"—P. C.—because it's an expression, not a name.) If the abbreviation is one word abbreviated by capital letters (such as TV, or NW for northwest), don't use a period. If an acronym has become so widely used that it's no longer considered an abbreviation, use lower-case letters (radar, snafu).
- If a word is abbreviated by two or more letters, use a period (Esq., Ph. D.).
- In informal writing, you may contract long words by using an apostrophe (sec'y) or abbreviate them with a period (Pres. or bldg.). Do not use this type of abbreviation in formal business writing.

When should you capitalize abbreviations?

- An abbreviated word of two or more letters should be capitalized if you would capitalize the spelled out word (Penn.) but not if the word is not ordinarily capitalized (fig.).
- Capitalize any abbreviation that combines the initials of two or more words (CBS).
- Do not capitalize Latin abbreviations (etc., op. cit., ibid.).

When should you use symbols instead of words?

The short answer is, "rarely." Use the dollar or pound signs with any number 10 or greater ($50; 50£). You may use % with any number 10 or greater, but with smaller numbers you should spell out "percent." (Yes, "per cent" and "percent" are acceptable!) Use the "each" symbol (@) only in billing situations (socks, 144 pairs @ $25). Do not use the ampersand (&) unless it's part of a company name (Dewey, Cheatam & Howe).

Irregular Abbreviations

You will encounter a few abbreviations that don't seem to relate to the word they're abbreviating. These will just have to be learned as you encounter them. Some of the most common are:

pp. (pages)

cc: Bob Smith (I sent a copy of this document to Bob Smith.)

viz: (namely)

i. e. (in other words)

et al. (and others)

e. g. (for example)

etc. (and the rest)

et seq. (and those that came after)

How to Write Numbers

Cardinal numbers 10 and above and ordinal numbers 10th and above should be written in numeral form except at the start of a sentence. Spell out cardinal numbers one through nine and ordinal numbers first through ninth, unless they are part of an address (3 Morningside Dr.), a recipe (5 cups flour) or a date (Dec. 9).

- Round numbers (five thousand, twenty million) should usually be spelled out.
- In general, all numbers in addresses should be expressed as numerals. (An exception is made in New York City, where streets are written as numerals and avenues are spelled out—215 E. 26th St., but 1120 Sixth Ave.)
- Use hyphens when spelling out fractions (two-thirds), numbers or parts of numbers between 21 and 99—but not in spelling out hundreds, thousands or millions.

Sixty-seven.

One hundred thirty.

One hundred thirty-one.

Six million, four hundred twenty-nine thousand, eight hundred ninety-eight.

- Hyphenate numbers and the unit of measurement if they're being used as modifiers, except when the measurement is "percent":

  She had an 18-inch waist.

  but

  We experienced a five percent sales gain.

  and

  Her waist measured 18 inches.

- Repeat symbols (The salary range is $30,000 to $40,000), but don't repeat spelled out units of measurement (The salary range is thirty to forty thousand dollars).

- You may use a decimal point to express numbers greater than one million (6. 8 million) if there are no more than two digits following the decimal point.

- Always spell out a number if it begins a sentence.

- If two numbers stand next to each other in a sentence, spell out one of the numbers. Which one you spell out is up to you: In general, you should spell the number that's easier to read.

- Insert a comma after every third digit, reading right–to–left (38,445; 3,222). Do not use commas following a decimal point (56,102. 3888). Do not use a comma if you're expressing a year (1996).

- Days of the month require a comma if they're placed after the month (December 25, 1956) but not if they're placed before the month (9 July 1850). Either style is acceptable. However, do not use the all-numerical form (6/11/93), as nobody will know whether you've put the month or the day first! Use ordinal numbers (August 15th) only if the date doesn't include a year.

- Time of day is usually spelled out if it's a full, half or quarter hour (Four o'clock in the afternoon; a quarter to noon), but written in numeral form otherwise (2:11 a. m.). Military time uses no punctuation (1800 hours, or simply 1800).

Roman Numerals

You'll seldom have to use or read Roman numerals in a business situation, except perhaps in writing outlines, but here's a quick course in how to translate Arabic to Roman:

Arabic	Roman	Arabic	Roman
1	I	15	XV
2	II	20	XX
3	III	40	XL
4	IV	50	L
5	V	60	LX
6	VI	90	XC
7	VII	100	C
8	VIII	500	D
9	IX	1000	M
10	X		

Note that you simply add Is, Vs or Xs, as appropriate, unless the number you're trying to express is one less, five less or 10 less than a multiple of five, 10, 50, 100, 500 or 1,000. In that case, place the difference between the number you're expressing, and the greater multiple. For instance, 48 would be written XLVIII; 49 is IL. Eighty-three is LXXXIII; 84 is LXXXIV. The year 1995 would be written MVM; next year it will be MXMVI. Now do you wonder why Roman numerals have hardly been used for centuries?

EXERCISES

Punctuation

I. Punctuate the following sentences:

1. Ive had some tough times in the past two years but that was the toughest day of my life

2. On the Senate floor one of the Republican partys major bills is in trouble The Democrats in the Appropriations Committee which must approve it seem intent on talking the bill to death

3. We're talking about the right to know making sure people have access to the information they want in a timely manner and in a form they can understand

4. Although it was thought to be broadly accurate Bede's history was written almost 300 years after the events it describes which is rather like us writing a history of Elizabethan England based on hearsay

5. Oddly McCormick never called for two of the most common shortenings tho and thru He just didnt like them which of course is all the reason that is necessary when its your newspaper

6. Websters first work A *Grammatical Institute of the English Language* consisting of three books a grammar a reader and a speller appeared between 1783 and 1785 but he didnt capture the publics attention until the publication in 1788 of *The American Spelling Book*

7. Outside the New College chapel Spooner rebuked a student by saying I thought you read the lesson badly today   But Sir I didnt read the lesson protested the student   Ah said Spooner I thought you didnt

II. Some of the following sentences could be punctuated better, and some are acceptable as they are. Find and correct the mistakes:

1. Before the Windsors' honeymoon was half over, the Devil, in the plausible guise of Charles Bedaux, had devised a sorry piece of work for the brother whom George VI had unwisely left in idleness.

2. The Duke did not care for Maxim's and the Tour d'Argent; they were the most celebrated restaurants but also the most expensive.

3. Reporters temperamentally and traditionally are skeptical and perhaps justifiably so, whenever the personal honesty of a public official is questioned.

4. At 6:45 (still 15 minutes before poll-closing time in the West) Eric Sevareid of CBS reported; "We are pretty confident now of a Kennedy victory; all of the computing machines are now saying Kennedy. "

5. If you're watching a black and white movie, its actually better to have a black and white television.

6. "Do you think he's innocent," the lawyer asked?

7. In the entire history of the case, both before the Committee on

Un-American Activities and in Hiss's two trials for perjury, no one could be found who could remember George Crosley—except Patricia Hiss.

Plurals, Possessives, Abbreviations, Capitalizations

Some of the following sentences contain mistakes. Identify and correct them:

1. I'll be arriving on Fri. , Aug 18, 1995.

2. "Keeping up with the Joneses'" is an old expression.

3. Pres. Bush was once the head of the C. I. A.

4. Woodrow Wilson was the only President of the United States to have a P. H. D. Degree.

5. Phenomenon such as comets and eclipses happen rarely.

6. One of my favorite reference books is the Reader's Encyclopedia.

7. I was praying with my Brethren from the Universal Life Church.

8. Mick Jagger is the Rolling Stones' most famous member.

9. Many americans love comedy shows from overseas, such as *Monty Python's Flying Circus.*

10. I spoke for several hours with Professor Einstein, who explained that his Theory of Relativity was just a wild guess.

11. A Muslim may have as many as four wives.

Numbers

Write out these numbers:

36,616;
406;
26.65;
6 7/8;
1,086,924.5

CHAPTER 3

Getting to Work

Editing and Proofreading

Basic editing primarily involves checking a manuscript for organization, grammar, spelling, punctuation, stylistic consistency and factual accuracy, and may involve extensive rewriting or "cutting and pasting." Proofreading involves working with material that's already typeset, checking it against the original manuscript.

In other words, editing mainly involves working on the big picture; proofreading is the correction of tiny details.

Editing, of course, involves the proofreading of a manuscript, and typeset copy often requires additional organizing or rewriting. Besides, nowadays, a lot of publishing gets done in-house, often with the same person handling the entire job. Therefore, editing and proofreading are really one ongoing, multi-step process.

Whether you're editing or proofreading, you'll need to know some standard proofreader's marks—that is, marks that tell the typesetter what corrections to make. The following list is not exhaustive, but it will get you through most situations.

PROOFREADERS' MARKS		
ℰ delete	ᵃ	capitalize
⌣ close the space	*a.m.*	set as small capitals
∧ insert here (plus word or character to be inserted)	Ɓⁱ⁴⁴	set lower case
# insert a space	*Bill*	set italic
b.b. bad word break	*Bill*	set roman
stet. let it stand; ignore	**Bill**	set bold
∽ transpose	=	insert hyphen
∟ move to left	⁻⁄ₙ	insert short (en) dash
⌐ move to right	⫫	insert long (em) dash
¶ new paragraph	*nr₂*	superscript
④ spell it out	H₂O	subscript
(four) set as a numeral	⌐*word*⌐	center in space
	⊗	period

Here's an example of how proofread copy might look:

Most men don't dress well especially for business and it's not
entirely their fault. Surveys show that more than three quarters of
American men don't buy their own clothes. Their wives, mothers,
or girlfriends do it for them! *stet*

Unfortunately, many women haven't the first notion of how to dress
a man. They'll choose ties that make a guy look like a circus freak, on
the grounds that classic stripes and polka-dots are "boring." Instead
of steering a fellow into a conservative business suit that will last him
twenty years, they'll dress him in something "stylish" that he'll have
to give to Goodwill after one season. They'll mix plaids and (paisle-) *b.b.*
ys until the poor guy looks like he's wearing a jambalaya!

Proofreading and editing require tremendous precision and attention
to detail. When you're proofreading, you'll have to read line-by-line,
breaking each line up into individual words, and sometimes individual
numbers and letters!

Many good proofreaders will read a piece of copy several times. First,
they'll glance over it quickly to see if any mistakes pop out at them.
Second, they'll read it very closely, looking for the harder-to-find mistakes in spelling, punctuation or grammar. (A good idea is to use a ruler
or a bookmark to keep the eye focused on individual lines during this
process. A proofreader should never take in a whole sentence or paragraph at a time, as you might do when reading for pleasure.)

Often, good proofreaders will check the typeset document against the original if they're in doubt about a spelling, punctuation or sentence structure.

Third, they'll read the typeset document carefully for content, making
sure that its meaning is clear, that it contains all necessary information
and references, and that there are no repetitions.

(Since you'll often be working with word-processed documents, you're likely to
find frequent repetitions: Sometimes, for instance, the author will want to
replace one paragraph with another and forget to delete the original paragraph.)

Do not trust the spell- and grammar-checking software in your computer!
You may use it to scan the copy before you proofread it yourself, but no
computer is as accurate as a good human proofreader. The main problem

with your computer's spell-checker is that if you misspell a word, but the spelling is also a word (such as "were" when you meant to write "where"), the computer won't catch it. Grammar-checking programs tend to be inflexible, and have no understanding of context. If they can't understand the context, they can't correct your grammar.

PROOFREADING TIPS:

- Pay special attention to elements such as headlines, sub-heads, call-out boxes and photo captions. These are the parts of a document that are certain to be read, so they've got to be perfect.

- Be particularly careful about names, titles and dates. Probably the worst proofreading mistake you can make is to misspell someone's name.

- Check all small elements such as page numbers and "running copy," such as the title of the report, which might appear centered at the top of each page, or the name and date of the newsletter, which might appear in the bottom outside corner of each page.

- Check all word breaks at the ends of lines (ex-tra, not ext-ra).

- If you're proofreading a document for the second time, check all the mistakes you caught the first time, to be sure the typesetter corrected them.

EDITING TIPS:

Check every sentence for grammar:

- Is each sentence complete, with a subject and a predicate?
- Does the subject agree with the verb?
- Does each clause have a referent?
- Does each modifier or participle have a referent?

Be sure the sentence conforms to your style book. Check to see:

Is every word spelled correctly?

Is the capitalization consistent?

Is the sentence punctuated in accordance with your style book?

Double-check all names and numbers:

Is every name spelled correctly?

Is every title correct?

Is every date correct?

Are all other numbers correct?

If the document involves mathematical equations, are they correct?

Watch for sloppy writing:

Does the same word appear too frequently?

Does the writer use too many clichés or too much jargon?

Does the writer use too-wordy constructions, like "It is to be hoped that..."?

- Check each sentence, each paragraph, and the entire document for organization. Are these elements put together in a logical, orderly manner? Is reading this document a "smooth and easy journey"?

Above all, does this document observe the One Big Rule?

If you're editing your own work, you should make all the changes you think necessary. If you're editing someone else's work, don't make any changes unless you've been authorized to do so. Instead, note all changes you propose to make, then get the author's permission to make them.

In the final stages of production, it's always a good idea to have more than one pair of eyes on any document. If you can get a colleague to proofread your work before you send it out or publish it, do so!

The Fog Index: A Never-Fail Key to Readability

In business, whatever you're writing has to be easy to read. The two biggest enemies of easy reading are long words and long sentences. You can't eliminate all long words and sentences, of course. But too many of them will make your document "foggy."

Many business writers use a formula called the "Fog Index" to help them write clear, concise reports, memos and letters. Learn to use the Fog Index immediately! You'll be amazed at how much it will improve your writing skills.

The Fog Index is a way of determining the reading level of a document. If a document is written at, say, a 10th-grade level, it means that an average 10th-grade student would be able to read and understand it easily.

Most experts agree that business reports and articles should be at about the 11th- or 12th-grade level of readability, although some very technical documents may be written at a higher level.

The Fog Index is only a guideline. For instance, if you find that your report is slightly above the 12th-grade level, it's not necessarily a problem. And, of course, many other factors go into the writing of a good report. Short words and sentences usually help, but so does "punchy" language; so do numbers; so do common words in place of jargon.

Also, it's not true that the more readable a report is, the better. If you write at the third-grade level, you'll sound like you're talking down to your readers—and that's never very effective.

The Fog Index is a mathematical formula, which you can use for any piece of writing other than poetry. Here's how it works:

1. Select a passage at random from your document. (You might want to choose three or more passages—for instance, the opening, a portion of the middle, and the conclusion.)

2. Count 100 consecutive words from that sample passage. Include all words except numbers that aren't written out. Contractions and hyphenated words count as one word.

3. Count the number of sentences in that passage, and divide the 100 words by that number. This will give you the average number of words per sentence. (For instance, if there are four sentences in those 100 words, divide 100 by four. The average number of words per sentence is 25.)

4. Count the number of words of three or more syllables in the passage, not counting proper names, and not counting words of which the third syllable is ing, es or ed.

5. Add the number of long words in the passage to the average number of words per sentence. (For instance, 25 words per sentence + 16 long words = 41.)

6. Divide this number by 10. (In this example, the result is 4.1.)

7. Multiply that result by four. (Here, the result is 16.4—the reading level of an average college senior.) That's your Fog Index. An index of 16.4 is much too high for most business writing: You've got some editing to do!

Let's try applying the Fog Index to the first 100 words of a well-known piece of writing:

> Fourscore and seven years ago, our fathers brought forth on this continent a new nation, conceived in liberty, and dedicated to the proposition that all men are created equal. Now we are engaged in a great civil war, testing whether that nation, or any nation so conceived and so dedicated, can long endure. We are met on a great battlefield of that war. We have come to dedicate a portion of that field as a final resting-place for those who here gave their lives that that nation might live. It is altogether fitting and proper that we should do this.

You'll observe that the passage has eight long words—"continent," "liberty," "dedicated," "proposition," "dedicated" again, "battlefield," "dedicate," and "resting-place," which counts as one word of three syllables. "Created" doesn't count, because without the ed suffix it would be a two-syllable word. The passage has five sentences.

So, here's the math:

> 100 / 5 (the number of sentences) = 20 (average number of words per sentence)
>
> 20 + 8 = 28
>
> 28 / 10 = 2.8
>
> 2.8 x 4 = 11.2

Abraham Lincoln wrote his Gettysburg Address at an 11th-grade level—perfect!

Let's do it again, with a piece of business writing:

> What bothers supporters of the market system is their fear that both clerical and lay critics have become more than society's social conscience: They've become the voice of a leftish ideolgy and unknowing supporters of people committed to increasing their own dominance over others. Sociologist William Boothby called the non-ecclesiastical critics the Useless Class who got their livelihood from the information industry and their power through manipulation of words rather than the making of things. Boothby cited the Small Companies Administration as the perfect example of how ideologues establish a power base within the federal government while simultaneously gleaning profits from policing certain occupations.

This 104-word passage contains 17 words (don't count "Small Companies

Administration" since that's a proper name), and has three sentences. Rounding off the fractions, here's the math:

104 words/3 sentences = 35 words per sentence

35 + 17 long words = 52

52/10 = 5.2

5.2 x 4 = 20.8

With a Fog Index of 20.8, this passage would be mighty hard going for anyone!

To de-fog this passage, you need to do only a few things, and they're easy:

• Take out words you don't need;

• Substitute short words for some of the long ones;

• Break long sentences into two or more short ones.

Let's start by striking out unnecessary words:

> Supporters of the market system fear that both church and lay critics have moved beyond being society's social conscience to become the voice of a leftish ideology and unknowing supporters of groups committed to increasing their own political power. Sociologist William Boothby called these critics the Useless Class who derived their livelihood from the information industry and their power through manipulating symbols rather than making things. Boothby cited the Small Companies Administration as the perfect example of how ideologues establish power within the federal government while profiting from policing certain occupations.

Now, we'll change some long words to short ones:

> People who support the market system fear that both church and lay critics have moved beyond being society's social conscience to become the voice of a leftish ideology and unknowing supporters of groups trying to increase their own political power. Sociologist Wiliam Boothby called these critics the Useless Class who made a living from the information industry and got power by manipulating symbols rather than making things. Boothby cited the Small Companies Administration as the perfect example of how such people gain power in the federal government while profiting from policing certain occupations.

Finally, we'll break up those long sentences:

> People who support the market system fear that both church and lay critics have moved beyond being society's social conscience. These critics, they say, have become the voice of a leftish ideology. Further, they're unknowing supporters of groups that are trying to increase their own political power. Sociologist William Boothby called these critics the Useless Class. This Useless Class makes a living from the information industry and gets power by twisting symbols rather than making things. Boothby cited the Small Companies Administration as the perfect example of how such people gain power in the federal government while profiting from policing certain occupations.

Now, this passage still has 103 words, but it contains six sentences and only 11 long words. Once again, here's the math:

$$103/6 = 17$$
$$17 + 11 = 28$$
$$28/10 = 2.8$$
$$2.8 \times 4 = 11.2$$

The passage is now at about the right reading level for most businesspeople.

MORE TIPS

• If you can cut a word out, cut it out.

• If a short word will do as well as a long one, use the short one.

• Use contractions, such as "you're," "he'd" and isn't."

• Avoid using sentences beginning with "There is," or "It is."

• Use the active voice (Jane closed the window), rather than the passive voice (The window was closed by Jane).

• Be careful of words with suffixes such as er, ent, ing, ion, orize. (For instance, take the sentence, "Following his oration, he was lionized by the entire population of the community." Clearer is, "After his speech, the whole town treated him as a hero.")

• Don't overuse "that" as a conjunction. "I think he's lying," is clearer than, "I think that he is lying."

Many software programs come equipped with programs that will enable you to measure the Fog Index of your writing. Some will even analyze and determine grade level for you.

Memos

The purpose of a memo is to get something done—to get someone to take action, to change people's opinions, to provide information that will stir things up. The keys to writing effective memos are:

• Organization

• Complete, accurate information

• Forceful style

Memos are usually internal documents—meant for your colleagues—but you'll occasionally write them for people outside the company, such as vendors or customers.

Memos are usually short, although there are no rules as to length. They often place less emphasis on information and more on exhortation. And they are frequently addressed to several people at once.

ORGANIZATION

How you organize a memo depends on the subject and on who will be reading it. But however you organize the memo, keep these three objectives in mind:

• Tell the readers exactly what they need to know—no more, no less;

• Explain this information;

• Tell them what you want them to do, and when to do it.

A well-organized memo will answer all immediately relevant questions concerning its subject. To supply those answers as clearly as possible, it will usually contain, at the bare-bones level, an introduction, a main body, recommendations and a conclusion.

A well-organized memo must also be well-reasoned. If your logic isn't good, you won't persuade anyone. If your memo is going to say, "We know A and B, and from that we must conclude C," you'd better be sure that C follows from A and B. For instance, a manager once circulated the following memo: "Yesterday, someone spilled iced tea on the carpet of the employee lounge, causing a permanent stain. Therefore, iced tea may no longer be drunk in carpeted areas." At least the manager gave everyone a good laugh: He was apparently the only one in the office who thought that the fact that the beverage was iced tea had anything to do with its being spilled on the rug.

When you're writing a memo, mention everything you want done, and all information that you have that will help the reader do it. Organize this information in a sensible sequence, so that the reader won't have to organize it himself.

You might use any one of several ways to organize information, depending on the kind of memo you're writing. Here are a few methods:

- **Chronological**: "First A happened, then B, then C, and now D. Therefore, we must do E."

- **Big picture to smaller pictures:** "Our manufacturing division has been sold to the Very Big Corp. of America. Its operation on our premises will cease at end of business Friday, June 30. Very Big will offer employment at the same or higher salaries to all management personnel in the division who wish to relocate to Very Big's offices in Cleveland. We will make every effort to absorb non-management personnel into other divisions. Those who cannot be absorbed will receive three months' salary as severance, dating from June 30."

- **Cause and effect:** "So that employees may attend the memorial service for Clara Belle, the office will close at 3 p.m. tomorrow."

- **Effect and cause:** "We're having a party! Our company president, Allbright Green, has declared tomorrow 'Goof Off and Do Nothing Day,' to celebrate the birth of puppies to his dog Brandy!"

- **Questions and answers:** "Are we really going out of business? No. Are we going to be laying off employees? Unfortunately, yes. Will the layoffs affect all departments? No, only the manufacturing divisions. When will these layoffs happen? We will inform all employees to be laid off by end of business today. If you don't hear further from us by quitting time, you can assume you're still employed."

- **Act I, Act II, Act III:** Just like a play, you state the problem, analyze it, and solve it, in that order. "Recently, A, B and C have happened. This means D, E, F and G. Therefore, we must do H, I and J."

- **Description:** "Donald Duck has just joined our company as senior vice president of customer service. He will be in charge of teaching customer service reps to lose their tempers and talk in loud, squawking voices."

THE FORM

Always write memos on company stationery. Beneath the company letterhead, use the following form:

> To: Frank Furter
>
> From: Olive Green
>
> Subject: Company Picnic
>
> Date: August 25, 1996

If you're sending the memo to fewer than 10 people, list all names after To:, but if you're sending it to a lot more people, you might prefer to write, "See distribution list" next to To:, and place the distribution list at the end of the memo. If you're sending the memo to a specific group of people, you may write "To: All Employees," or "To: Manufacturing Staff." Next to Subject:, use as few words as possible.

You may include your phone extension next to your name. If your company's a large one, and the recipient is in another department, you might include his department next to his name.

HOW SHOULD YOU WRITE IT?

A memo longer than two pages should open with an introduction, preferably of five to 10 lines. You should write the introduction after you've written the main body of the memo, in the plainest possible language. This will make it easier for your readers to understand a long, complicated memo, or to skim over the memo and read only the parts that apply to them. Although a summary can't supply all the facts, it should give the overall meaning of the memo and highlight the central idea.

If you expect the memo to be good news to the reader, the introduction should contain a summary of the information in the main body. That way, you immediately alert the reader that there's something good coming up. The summary should include findings, conclusions and recommendations. If you can keep the summary to no more than 10 lines, include a brief overview of important details.

However, if you expect an unfavorable reaction to your memo, the introducton should simply state the problem or the situation. Save your findings, conclusions and recommendations for the end of the memo, by which time (with any luck) you'll have prepared the reader to accept your opinions.

In many cases, the introduction should begin with a reference to some past meeting or other contact, such as, "Thanks again for all the good advice you gave us yesterday," or might begin with a question: "Do you want to help raise everyone's salary?"

The main body of the memo contains the facts and explains what they mean. This could be a plain statement, requiring no more than two sentences, or it could include several pages of analysis. Here is where you put all the facts the reader needs to understand your position or to do what you want him to do. It's also where you persuade the reader to do what you want him to do, if necessary.

In the main body, you'll want to organize the information in one of the ways described above. For easier reading, you could begin each paragraph or each idea with a heading, such as "Objectives," "Progress So Far," "Options," "Resources We'll Require," "Possible Problems," "and "Recommendations."

The conclusion wraps up the information in the introduction and main body. If the memo is short and easy to understand, a conclusion may not be necessary.

In the conclusion, you should stress the objective of the project under discussion, the main points of information, and your directive or recommendation, in a tone that will impart the proper attitude to the reader. Include the deadline for action, if there is one; acknowledgement of any actions already taken; and a sentence or two of "pep." For instance:

> When we've compiled a comprehensive, fully cross-referenced directory of our customer base, our sales and speed of fulfillment should both rise dramatically. We've already got almost all of the information we need to put this directory together. Now, we just need your recommendations on how best to cross-reference the entries. We need your input by noon tomorrow. Our thanks to all of you for all the good work you've done so far on this project. It's going really well, and we should have it wrapped up and ready to deliver by the weekend!

WHO SHOULD RECEIVE THE MEMO?

A memo can go to one person or to everyone in the company. When deciding who should receive a copy, simply ask yourself, "Does this person need to know this?" If the memo involves an idea that you want to be sure to get credit for, send it to two or more people. That way, there can be no doubt that it's yours.

Letters

No two people will ever agree on exactly what is the proper format for a letter. Many different formats are acceptable. The following format is standard and quite conservative, and is acceptable for any business letter, formal or informal:

```
        THE VERY BIG CORPORATION OF AMERICA
                   215 E. 26th St.
                  New York, N.Y. 10010
                   (212) 555-1212

January 1, 1999

Ms. Xxx Xxxxxx
Xxxxxxx Xxxxxxx
Xxxxxx, Xxx.

Dear Ms. Xxxxxx:

Xxxxxxxx xxx xxx xxxxxxx. Xxxxx xx xxx x xx xxxxxxxx.
Xxxxxxxxxxxx xx x xxxx xxxx, xx xxxxx xxxx xxxxx xxxxx
xxxxxxx xx xxxxx xxxxxx, xx xxxxx xx xxx xxxxxxx xx x xxx.

Xxxxxxx xx xxxxx xxxx xxxxx xxxxx x xx xxx, xxxxx xxx
xxxxxxx x xxxxx, xxxx xx xxxxxx. Xxx 000,000 xxx, xxxx.
Xxxxxxxxxx x xxxx x xxxx xxx xx xxxxxxxxx. X xxxx xxx xxxx
xxxxxxxxx, xx xxxxx xxxxxxx xxxxxxxxx.

X xxx Xxxxx Xxxxxx, xxx xxx xxxxxxx xxxxxxx. X xxxxx.

Sincerely,

Geraldine Snooks
Executive Vice President
```

The centered copy at the top of the page is the letterhead. This will almost always be pre-printed on the paper you're using. Just below that is the date. The date may be flushed left, or to the right of the letterhead:

January 1, 1999   January 1, 1999

Below the date is the **inside address.** The inside address is always flushed left. Some authorities say that the inside address should have four lines:

> Mr. John Q. Businessman
> The Small-Town Brokerage
> 123 West 456th St.
> Anytown, IL 56789

Other authorities prefer a three-line inside address, leaving out the street address and the ZIP code and using the old-fashioned state abbreviation:

> Ms. Euphemia Andrew
> Larks Unlimited
> Athol, Mass.

Next comes the **salutation.** In business letters, this almost always consists of three words: "Dear," the addressee's title, and the addressee's surname, followed by a colon:

> Dear Dr. Howard:

Say "Dear" even if it's a hostile letter.

In very informal letters, you may use the recipient's first name, followed by a comma instead of a colon:

> Dear Dave,

If you're being very formal, you may choose to say, "Dear Sir:" or "Dear Madame:" instead of a surname. However, this will sound very impersonal.

Actually, only in very rare cases should you write a letter to someone whose name you don't know. If you don't know the name or title of the person you want to address, find it out before you write the letter!

If it's exceptionally inconvenient to do this, or if the letter is not addressed to any person or organization (such as a letter of recommendation), you may use one of the following salutations:

> Dear Madame or Sir:

> Ladies and Gentlemen:

"To whom it may concern" is not recommended.

You may lay out the **body** of the letter in one of two ways. Most businesspeople prefer to leave an extra line between paragraphs, and not indent a new paragraph, as in the example above. Some writers don't leave a line between paragraphs, and indent each new paragraph. Either format is acceptable, although the former method looks more businesslike.

Following the body comes the complimentary close and the signature. These can be flushed left or aligned under the date (when it is to the right of the letterhead):

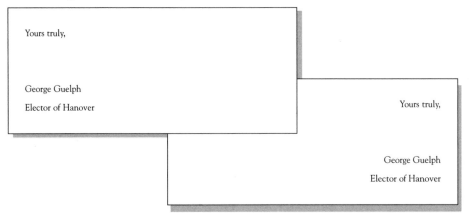

Yours truly,

George Guelph
Elector of Hanover

Yours truly,

George Guelph
Elector of Hanover

In a formal business letter, you will usually use a complimentary close such as "Yours truly," or "Sincerely." However, you'll find that the complimentary close you choose can give a subtle flavoring to the tone of the letter. A very friendly letter might close with:

> Best personal regards,
> Warmest regards,
> As ever,
> All the best,

To strike a very formal tone, you might use one of these:

> Respectfully yours,
> Very truly yours,
> Yours faithfully,

Leave three or four lines below the complimentary close, to make room for the signature. Type the name of the writer (yours or another's) and, below that, the sender's title:

> Homer Samuel
> Manager, Purchasing

If there are two signatures, place them side by side, with the higher-ranking signature to the left:

David Clark   Peter Stern
President   ExecutiveVice President

Two lines below the signature, flushed left, place the typist's initials, in lower-case letters. Below that line, place the notation "Enclosure" if you're enclosing materials in addition to the letter. If you're sending a copy of the letter to someone else, then type cc: [names of other recipients]:

tih

Enclosure

cc: Evelyn Hampster, Charles Farley

These final three lines are optional.

Job Descriptions

You should have up-to-date job descriptions on hand for every position in your department.

A job description is a list of the specific responsibilities and required skills for each position. Clarity is very important in writing job descriptions.

MAIN FUNCTIONS OF A JOB DESCRIPTION

- **To list duties that must be performed to accomplish departmental objectives.** Each job description in a department is a piece of a puzzle: If you put them all together, you'll have a good idea of how the department works as a team. Further, if you examine and revise all job descriptions in your department, you'll cover all tasks that need to be done, without hiring two people to do the same work.

- **To help you to hire the right person for the job.** If you have a complete list of the skills that the job requires, it'll be easier to make sure the applicant has what it takes.

- **To let the employee know exactly what is expected of him.** If it's listed on the job description, he'd better do it.

- **To make performance evaluations easier.** You can look at each point on a job description and ask yourself, "Is the employee doing this satisfactorily?" A written job description protects both employer and employee when there's a grievance over a performance evaluation.

However, the usefulness of a job description is zero if it's not updated every year or so, particularly if technological changes have altered the job's requirements. (If you've had the same job for even a couple of years, you know that the scope of your duties can change quickly.)

WRITING THE JOB DESCRIPTION

You'll need to employ different styles of writing to describe different types of jobs. A good generalization is that the more responsibility is attached to the job, the more the job description should focus on those responsibilities rather than on specific duties or skills. For example, you wouldn't write, on the company president's job description, "Arrive no later than 9:00 a.m.; hold no fewer than one sales meeting per week," etc. On the other hand, an entry-level clerk's job description would include specifics such as "put files in order at the end of each business day" and "distribute staff mail."

Before you write a job description, consult the employee who currently has the job and his or her manager. Both should list the job's responsibilities and skill requirements. The manager should add information on how this job fits in with the department's and the company's overall objectives, and should discuss how the job has changed recently and might change in the near future. The employee should list everything he does in relation to his job, then determine which of those things is an actual requirement of the job, and what skills are needed to fulfill those requirements.

In organizing the job description, you might use one of two methods:

- Write the most important or most frequently performed duty first, then the second-most important, then the third. This is particularly useful if the job is mainly repetitive, such as assembly line work or telemarketing.

- Write the duties in order. ("Edit each form; divide forms into three stacks—priority, deferred, special—alphabetize each stack; deliver each stack to the data-entry clerk.") This system is most useful when the job is repetitive but involves several tasks.

You may write the job description in a narrative style, using complete sentences and paragraphs, or write it as a list, using bullets or numbers to set off each task. If you're using the "list" style, you need not use complete sentences—but be sure the information is as clear as can be.

Make it plain, in the job description, how the employee will be evaluated. If the employee will be evaluated mainly on the basis of one or two tasks or skills, be sure to mention this.

Here's one example of a job description:

> Job Title: Financial Aid Assistant
> Job Code Number: 0802
> Location: Financial Aid Office
> Date: January 1, 1996
> Reports to: Pansy Yonger, Financial Aid Officer
> Salary Range: $18-25,000
>
> Financial aid assistant is responsible for the accurate processing and filing of financial aid applications and for helping applicants to present accurate, readable applications.
>
> Under supervision of the financial aid officer, the financial aid assistant performs the following duties:
> - Opens and sorts all mail addressed to the financial aid office;
> - Examines, processes and sorts all financial aid applications before delivering them to the financial aid officer;
> - Answers applicant's questions on telephone, by letter or in person, as appropriate;
> - Explains application procedures to applicants and assists them in filling out application forms;
> - Maintains office's filing system;
> - Takes messages for financial aid officer;
> - Composes and types letters, reports and memos at the direction of the finanicial aid officer;
> - Assists financial aid officer in determining disposition of financial aid applications.
>
> Skills Required:
> Type 40 wpm; HS diploma or equivalent; strong command of English; working knowledge of Spanish; alphabetizing; filing.

Reports

A report can be of any length, from one page to thousands of pages. It can be a plain statement of facts, or it can include exhaustive documentation and analysis.

You'll know the objective of the report before you begin to research or write it. Whether the objective is to address a problem or to simply publish information, keep the objective in mind as you do the research and decide what you're going to say. Don't let yourself go off on a tangent, unless you're convinced that doing so will force a major change in your favor.

To put it another way, if you set out to mine for silver, set all your intelligence and all your energies towards the objective of mining for silver. Don't let anything distract you. But if, while mining for silver, you strike gold, your new objective will be to mine for gold!

Be steadfast in your objective, but flexible in your conclusions. If you're writing a long report that requires a lot of research, you'll probably have some preconceived ideas of what your conclusions will be. That's fine, but it's likely that you'll make some discoveries in the course of your research that will force you to some other, unexpected conclusions.

Usually, you'll want to outline the report before you write it. This is especially important if it's a long report that contains a lot of complicated information. If you don't have a good idea of how the report is going to flow, you risk writing it in a disjointed manner, jumping from one point to another.

Most reports are fairly straightforward in terms of organization. Usually, you'll want to start by stating the problem or objective that the report will address; you might also want to give a brief outline of your conclusions and recommendations. After all, a report isn't a novel; you shouldn't surprise the reader at the end.

How you organize the information in the main body of the report will be largely up to you. Most writers prefer to determine the main points they want to address, and the minor points that grow out of each major point, and organize the main body of the report something like this:

Part I:

    a. Broad overview of most important point (A).

    b. Closer examination of point A, with broad overview of point A's sub-points.

    c. Closer examination of A's sub-points.

    d. Preliminary conclusions based on analysis of A.

Part II:

    a. Broad overview of second-most important point (B).

    b. Closer examination of point B, with broad overview of point B's sub-points.

    c. Closer examination of B's sub-points.

    d. Preliminary conclusions based on analysis of B.

And so on, until you've come to the final section of the report, which will include your conclusions and recommendations.

FORMAT

Many reports are actually memos or letters, and may be written in the letter or memo style. A longer report may contain various elements in addition to a plain statement of information and require a more complex format.

A formal report may contain any of the following elements, usually in the following order, although it's up to the author to determine which of these elements are necessary:

- **Cover.** A long, formal report should have a cover, rather than simply being stapled together. The cover can be simple or elaborate, but in any case should be neat and attractive, and should bear the title of the report and (usually) the author's name.

- **Flyleaf.** A blank page that precedes all other pages, the flyleaf is like a handkerchief in a man's breast pocket: It has no purpose but to dress things up.

- **Title fly.** This is just like the flyleaf, except that it contains the title of the report (but not the author's name) centered on the page.

- **Title page.** The title page contains the title, the author's name, and perhaps the author's company, department and address.

- **Letter of authorization.** This is a copy of the letter you received, authorizing you to write the report. If you received no such letter, you might wish to mention your authorization in the foreword or in the letter of transmittal.

- **Letter of transmittal.** This is a letter that says, in effect, "Here's your report." It might include a summary of the report or a statement of its objectives, as well as thanks to anyone who was particularly helpful to the writing of the report.

- **Foreword.** This is much like a letter of transmittal, except that it's written in standard paragraph form, not in letter form. Usually, if you include a letter of transmittal, you won't need a foreword.

- **Acknowledgements.** If your list of people to thank is very long, you might want to put your acknowledgements on a separate page.

- **Table of contents.** This tells you on what page each section of the report begins. Many word-processing programs will generate a table for you, which you can then fine-tune to your specifications.

- **List of illustrations.** In effect, this is a table of contents covering only pictures (photographs, designs, drawings or reproductions).

- **List of figures, maps and tables.** It's common practice to list charts, graphs, maps and tables separately from pictures.

- **Summary.** You might choose to precede the report with a paragraph or two telling the reader, very briefly, what you're going to say. This is especially useful if the report is long and complex.

- **Body.** This is the report itself, however you've decided to organize it.

- **Appendix.** This contains brief, supplementary reports. For instance, if you were writing a report on American professional football, you might include an appendix on the Canadian Football League. You may want to include several appendices.

- **Footnotes.** The notes may appear at the bottom of the page where the referent occurs; at the end of each chapter; or in a section at the end of the report.

- **Glossary.** If the report contains a great many technical or foreign terms that most readers should know but some readers might not, it may be more practical to define those terms in a glossary, rather than interrupt the flow of the report to provide definitions.

- **Bibliography.** The bibliography lists all sources of information. The standard method of listing sources is alphabetically by author. Following the author's name, list the title, name of publisher or name and number of periodical, and date of publication:

> Manfred S. Guttmacher, M.D., *America's Last King*, Charles Scribner's Sons, 1941.
>
> Joseph Dobrian, "Dodging the Wild Beer Bottle," *Boxing Illustrated*, November 1984.

- **Index.** An index is hardly ever necessary to a report, unless the report is exceptionally long. Your word processing program will usually be able to make a serviceable index for you.

Press Releases

A press release is, in effect, a very short news article. It's what you send to newspapers, magazines and TV stations when there's something big happening at your company, in the hope that you'll get some press coverage.

A press release must observe the One Big Rule—and then some! It's got to be short, punchy, and absolutely accurate.

Usually, you should write a press release in what journalists call an "inverted pyramid": Place the most important point at the very beginning, followed by details directly relating to it, then list the other points in descending order of importance.

Answer all a journalist's "Big Six": who, what, when, where, why and how.

If the release contains numbers, put them at the top. Numbers grab the eye.

Normally, a press release should be written on special press release letterhead paper, which typically says "press release" at the top left, along with the name and phone number of someone to contact for more information.

The release should start with a headline (usually in all caps), followed by a dateline.

Here is an example:

>>>>>>>>>>> PRESS RELEASE >>>>>>>>>>>>
Contact: Ovid G. Wotasnozzle (216) 933-3333

BATTENBERG IS NEW PRESIDENT OF VERY BIG

CLEVELAND, July 9, 1997—Louis Battenberg has been appointed president of the Very Big Corporation of America, based here, effective August 1. He succeeds William Hamilton, who will retire at the end of this month.

Battenberg, who has served as Very Big's executive vice president since 1990, joined Very Big in 1980 as vice president of sales. Prior to joining Very Big, he was vice president of The Medium-Sized Co., Inc.

"I'm thrilled that I've been called on to lead Very Big into the 21st century," Battenberg stated. "I expect to preside over years of steady and rapid growth."

Hamilton has been president of Very Big since 1975. He joined the company as a stock boy in 1941.

"This was the grandest job in the world, and watching this company change and grow over the past 56 years was an experience I wouldn't trade for anything," Hamilton remarked in announcing his retirement.

For more information, or to arrange interviews with Mr. Battenberg or Mr. Hamilton, contact Ovid G. Wotasnozzle at (216) 933-3333.

Note that the press release could stand as a short newspaper article: An editor could simply type it into a computer, and it would be ready to be placed at the bottom of the business page.

EXERCISES

Proofreading:

I. Proofread and correct the following text. The subject matter may not interest you, but then many documents you proofread may be about topics of little interest.

> **Mhuammad Ali regained the Heavyweight Championship by defeating George Foreman in 1974. He lost thetitle toLeon Spinks in 1978 and regained it later that year. Following his, rematch with Spinks, he hinted that he was retiring. Over the next two years,**

the WBA and the WBC recognized different claimants as Ali's successor. In 1980, Ali "unretired"and made a come-back against the WBC claimant, Larry Holmes. Since the claim to the title was in dispute at that time. And since Ali hadnot lost his title int he ring, hemust be regarded as having been the defending champion—and Holmes, the challenger, in that fight.

Thus, intellectually honest historians generally agree that Holmes won the Heavyweight Championshipby defeeting Ali in nineteen-eighty. Since then, that title has changed hands in the following succession: Michael Spinks, Mike Tyson, James Douglas, Evander Holyfield, Riddick Bowe, Evander Holyfield, Michael Moorer, George Foreman. In each case, the title chagned hands in the ring; in no case was an elimination tournament involved.

While You might be right that the officials gave a bad decision in the Foreman-Schultz fight (and even that point is nowhere near so black-and-white as you'd have us believe), to argue that Forman has no leigitimate claim to the title is simply pernicious.

II. As you see from this list of ingredience, chef Jacques Pépin makes chocoate cake with almost no flour

12 ozs. semi-sweet choclate
11/2 sticks sweet butter, softened
8 large eggs
1 cup sugar
1 teaspoon grated orange rind
2 cups almonds ground in the blender (yields 21/4 cups ground)
1/2 cup fresh breadcrumbs (about one slice bread
1 cup heavy cream, whipped

Fog Index:

I. Calculate the Fog Index for the following 104-word passage:

The question was what Plimpton's death meant to Lachlan and Fairbanks. To the extent that the Lachlan campaign was aimed at winning at all, rather than at simply protesting, it had always depended heavily on coming through a broken field at the convention. Bob Jones, for one, had always felt that Lachlan's only serious chance would come at a convention deadlocked between

Plimpton and Fairbanks. His theory, expounded to many a skeptical delegate and journalist, was that Plimpton and Lachlan between them would stop Fairbanks, and that enough Fairbanks people would then switch to Lachlan, in preference to Plimpton, to give him the nomination.

II. Write about something unusual that happened to you at work in the past few days. Write at least 200 words—preferably more—and let the fog index be less than 12.

Memos:

Think of a book you've read recently that you feel would be helpful to your co-workers. (This could be a "how-to" book for business, a self-help or inspirational book, a biography of someone you admire, or a novel with an important message or an original idea.) Using any organizational style you please, write a memo to your boss addressing the following questions (although not necessarily in this order):

- **What is the book called?**
- **Who are the author and publisher?**
- **What is the book about?**
- **Why should everyone in the department read it?**
- **How can we apply the lessons of the book to the workplace?**
- **What specific profit—financial or psychological—will we gain from this book?**
- **Should we implement a group study of the book and its principles? If so, what form should this take?**
- **What are some of the book's principles that we can implement immediately?**

Job Descriptions:

I. Without looking at any job description that might actually exist, write your own job description.

II. Do the same for someone you know.

Press Releases:

I. Write a press release announcing something exciting that has just happened in your company. Using no more than 300 words, make the reader want to expand your release into a feature article.

II. Re-write the following press release to make it more interesting and readable:

PRESS RELEASE

Contact: William Gladstone (212) 779-8826

WRITER NEW OWNER OF METS

NEW YORK CITY, March 1, 1996—"Eighty million dollars was a small price to pay. I raised the money in just a few days by selling a few of my poems. We're going to win the pennant this year, and four years out of every five thereafter, indefinitely.

"I'm also going to build a new baseball park, probably near Wall St.," Joseph Dobrian revealed. "I'm going to move the Mets out of Shea Stadium as soon as I can."

Dobrian, a freelance writer who lives in Manhattan, announced that he has made a major purchase: the New York Mets baseball club. He said he made the purchase because he always wanted to have a major league baseball team.

The entire purchase price was reported to be $80 million.

Dobrian said he planned to release all Met players from their contracts and hire all new players. He will also change the team name to the New York Moderates.

For more information, contact William Gladstone at (212) 797-8826.

Getting to Be an Expert

Dos and Don'ts from the Experts

DOS:

- Write the subject and the verb, then worry about the rest. Say, "I left the office yesterday afternoon at about 3:00 to go to a seminar," not, "Yesterday afternoon, at about 3:00, since there was a seminar I had to go to, I left the office." Say, "The boss left early to go to a seminar," not "The boss, who had to go to a seminar, left early."

- Replace adverbs with snappy, dynamic verbs. "Sales rose very steeply last month" sounds okay, but your readers would probably rather read, "Sales soared last month."

- Use personal pronouns. "I will look into your complaint" is far stronger than "Your complaint will be looked into." In the first example, you're promising to assume responsibility. In the second, it sounds like you're saying, "*Somebody's* going to look into it." Who? Long ago, someone created the myth that personal pronouns are inappropriate to business writing. That idea is pure foolishness, and it's about time we got rid of it.

- Use clear, imaginative similes, metaphors and anthropomorphisms to pep up your writing. A *simile* is an expression that compares one thing to another, as in "The boss came out of his chair like a scorched ferret." You've written a m*etaphor* when you characterize, rather than compare, as in, "He's a real pussycat." An a*nthropomorphism* is when you attribute human characteristics to an animal or to an inanimate object, as in, "My invoice is growing a long gray beard."

However, be conservative with these expressions. They are the salt and pepper of writing, not the meat!

- Be aware of the connotations of certain words and phrases. Two words may mean the same thing, but one may have a much more positive connotation than the other. The philosopher Bertrand Russell provided the following examples: "I've got an eye for the ladies; you're a sex maniac. I'm prudent; you're timid. I'm a visionary; you're impractical. I'm an idealist; you're a radical."

- Be very careful of loaded phrases like "for your information," "please be advised," "obviously," and others that might anger or intimidate.

- Use small ones. If you can think of a short, plain, everyday word, use it—don't *utilize* it! But big words can be your friends at times. For instance, if you don't say *disestablishment*, you'll have to say, "changing the law so that the Church of England is no longer the state religion of England."

- Remember that technical terms have their places. If you're writing a scientific document, you're likely to use a lot of words that only scientists know. But the place to put a difficult word is in a simple, clear sentence.

- Use repetition for emphasis. Consider the following sentence: "My plan will lead to higher productivity, higher sales, higher margins, higher profits, higher consumer satisfaction and higher employee morale." It's a lot snappier than, "My plan will improve productivity, sales, margins, profits, consumer satisfaction and employee morale."

DON'TS

- Don't automatically cut out prepositions to shorten a sentence. "We need an updated accounts payable and receivable management system" is a shorter sentence than "We need to update our system for managing accounts payable and receivable." However, those prepositions make the second sentence easier to read!

- Don't over-qualify. For instance, don't say, "At the present time, I'm feeling optimistic about the project." "I'm feeling" already implies the present.

- Avoid phrases like "in this way" or "in a [such-and-such] manner." Instead of "He greeted me in a very friendly manner," say, "He gave me a friendly greeting."

- Seldom turn verbs into nouns. Instead of saying, "I will run a check on the system," say, "I will check the system." Instead of saying, "He was the first baseman and sometimes played catcher," say, "He played first base and sometimes caught."

- Beware of constructions that use *give, have, provide,* or similar verbs to turn another verb into a long, modified noun. Which is easier to read: "He had a negative reaction to my suggestion," or "He didn't like my suggestion"?

- Avoid using *there is* or *there are,* as in "There are reasons why I feel that way." "I have reasons for feeling that way" is clearer, because it stresses that the reasons are yours, not simply that they exist. However, some writers go overboard in their efforts to eliminate all *there is* constructions. A sentence like "There are gold deposits in my back yard" is okay, because you're trying to emphasize the gold deposits, not your back yard.

- Avoid redundancies. Beware of phrases like "past history" and "unwanted intruders." However, be certain that what looks like a redundancy doesn't actually provide a useful explanation. For instance, a phrase like "the state of New York" is acceptable if the reader might not otherwise know whether you mean the state or the city. "The Balkan country of Bulgaria" is acceptable if you're uncertain whether your readers know where Bulgaria is. But if you're writing to the Bulgarian ambassador, remember that he knows it's a Balkan country.

- Don't vary your terms for the sake of doing so. In other words, avoid sentences like, "Sales are down in Chicago, partly because residents of the Windy City have been staying indoors to beat the long heat wave that has blanketed Chi-town." Much more to the point is, "Sales are down in Chicago, partly because the heat wave there is keeping people indoors."

- Don't attach degrees to absolute terms. For instance, don't say "totally destroyed." If a thing is destroyed, the word "totally" is implied. Don't say, "a few short yards away." A yard is 36 inches, neither more nor less. Don't say, "partial suppression of free speech." That's like saying "a little bit pregnant."

Everyone's Favorite Mistakes

Observing imaginary rules. Many writers sacrifice clarity and brevity for the sake of "rules" that may not be rules at all.

There, I just broke one of them—I ended a sentence with a preposition! There is no such rule as "It's wrong to end a sentence with a preposition."

You shouldn't use a preposition at the end of a sentence if it doesn't belong in the sentence at all (as in, "Where's the library at?"), but there's nothing wrong with putting the preposition at the end if it belongs in the sentence. "Where did you come from?" is perfectly good English.

If you go out of your way to avoid ending a sentence with a preposition, your writing will often be too wordy and self-conscious. As Sir Winston Churchill once joked, "That is the kind of pedantry up with which we must not put!"

Another famous "rule" is that you must never split infinitives. (That is, if you're expressing a verb as an infinitive, such as "to speak," you mustn't separate the "to" from the verb. It's supposedly wrong to write a sentence such as "I'm going to carefully investigate this matter," because you've separated "to" and "investigate.")

In fact, the only problem with split infinitives is that they can sometimes lead to a too-elaborate, too-wordy style of writing. Both, "He tried to thoroughly explain the situation," and "He tried to explain the situation thoroughly" are standard, but the latter construction sounds a little odd, mainly because that isn't the way most people would say the sentence.

The real problem with split infinitives is that the words that you use to split them often ought not to be in the sentence at all! In the sentence above, for instance, the word "thoroughly" is just excess baggage. "He tried to explain the situation" is sufficient, because, after all, nobody assumes that his explanation was anything but thorough.

Overusing the passive voice. Writing or speaking in the "active voice" means that you describe someone doing something—like "Jane closed the window." The "passive voice" is a style that describes something having something done to it—like "The window was closed by Jane."

Businesspeople tend to use the passive voice a lot, probably because using it keeps you from having to use personal pronouns. (A popular but ridiculous rule states that personal pronouns—especially I—have no place in business writing.) However, it's usually a better idea to use the active voice.

The active voice is usually clearer, shorter and more interesting than the passive voice. Note, in the examples above, that the use of the passive voice increased the length of the sentence by 50 percent.

Compare the following two sentences:

> It is to be hoped that the suggestions submitted by our committee will be acted upon by your department.

> I hope your department will act on our committee's suggestions.

Just by using the passive voice, the writer of the first sentence manages to sound pompous, imperious, patronizing and downright rude. The writer of the second sentence sounds assertive but polite.

If you use the passive voice, you risk sounding evasive. "I made a mistake" is much more straightforward than, "A mistake was made."

At times, the passive voice will suit your needs better than the active. For instance, you might use the passive voice if the thing being acted upon is more important to the sentence than the person acting on it, as in "The report was very well received." Here, you want to make the point that the report did well; it's less important to name the people who received it.

Sentences written in the passive voice do tend to have a pleasant rhythm, and in some cases the passive voice will be clearer than the active. But when either voice will do, it's usually better to use the active voice.

Using clichés. "It has come to my attention that...". "Here's the bottom line." "Give me a ballpark figure." These overworked phrases aren't bad by definition. But if you use them at all, you'll be tempted to overuse them. That's how clichés get to be clichés.

I once worked in an office where, when an employee had a baby, the personnel department would circulate a memo saying something like, "Audrey Smith gave birth yesterday to a bouncing baby boy, Homer Israel Smith...". The names of the parents, and the name, weight and sex of the baby always changed, but the kid was always "bouncing."

Finally, a co-worker remarked that just once, he'd like someone to have a baby who landed with a *SPLAT*.

Of course, it's impossible to *completely* eliminate well-known figures of speech or overworked phrases. But be aware that they can detract from what you're trying to say.

Overusing jargon and euphemisms. A few people have the idea that using "office-ese" makes them sound more businesslike, and maybe even more powerful. Not so.

I once had a boss who asked us to "Place your time-sheets on that shelving unit there so that we can access them at the end of each pay period." She should have said, "Place your time-sheets on that shelf so we can pick them up on Friday."

Sending the *first draft* of an angry letter. When you have to write an angry letter or memo, go ahead and do it. Make it as vicious as you like. Call the person every name you've ever felt like calling him. Accuse him of every rotten thing you've ever suspected him of. Tell him exactly what you're going to do to him if you're ever in a position to do it.

When you've finished, put the letter in a drawer and leave it there until tomorrow morning. Then, read it once more to remind yourself of how much fun you had writing it, tear it up and write the real letter. It'll come out civilized, reasonable and telling—so much so that the person you're sending it to might even see things your way at last.

Using jokes and obscure references. We all think our own jokes are funny. But not everybody else is going to get them, and there's always a chance that someone will misunderstand one of your jokes in a disastrous way if you're not there to explain it. Jokes and obscure references are fine in personal letters or in creative writing, but in business writing, be *very* careful.

Using adjectives instead of adverbs. If someone plays the piano very loudly, don't say that he plays very loud. Adverbs (which often end in *ly*) modify verbs, such as, in this case, "plays." Adjectives only modify nouns.

Using adverbs instead of adjectives. Some writers, when using a "sense verb" (*taste, feel, look, smell, sound, think*), will modify it with an adverb instead of modifying the subject with an adjective. For instance:

> Whatever you're cooking, it smells deliciously.

Here, the writer mistakenly modifies the sense verb "smells," instead of the subject, "Whatever you're cooking." This subject is a compound noun, so you'd use an adjective (in this case, "delicious") to modify it.

However, consider this sentence, in which the adverb is properly used:

> She smelled deliciously of roses.

Here, the adverb, "deliciously," modifies the compound adverb "of roses," not the sense verb "smelled."

Misplacing modifiers. Even the best writers will sometimes confuse the reader by misplacing a modifier, or by punctuating it incorrectly, or by otherwise making it unclear what the modifier is, and what it's supposed to be modifying. Here are a few examples of how these foul-ups can happen.

> A car was reported stolen by Rev. Thomas yesterday.

Now, did Rev. Thomas report the car stolen, or did someone else report that the minister had stolen a car? Here's an example of how a writer can get into trouble by using the *passive voice* ("A car was reported..."). By changing the sentence to active voice ("Rev. Thomas reported yesterday that his car was stolen."), you've removed all confusion.

> Being a ferocious jungle creature, I knew that the tiger would be hard to make friends with.

Wait a minute! Are you a ferocious jungle creature? If you're not, the sentence should read, "I knew that the tiger, being a ferocious jungle creature, would be hard to make friends with."

> He bought the elephant, along with his sister.

And which did he pay more for, the elephant or his sister? Far better is "He and his sister bought the elephant."

Dangling participles and modifiers. When you write a participle (a verb ending in *ing*) or a modifying phrase that contains a verb, you need to be sure that that phrase or participle has a referent—a person or thing to which it refers. If it has no referent, it's called a "dangling" participle or modifier, and it can lead to a few laughs—at your expense.

> Having had a few drinks, the celebration became rather rowdy.

The celebration had a few drinks? It's better to say, "Since we'd had a few drinks, the celebration became rather rowdy," or, "Having had a few drinks, we became rather rowdy."

> The house comes into view, climbing the hill.

Here, we hope you mean "The house becomes visible as one climbs the hill." Otherwise, we've got to deal with a house, normally invisible to the naked eye, now reared up on its hind legs and struggling uphill as its image becomes more and more distinct.

> Having been told that she was a nincompoop, Ms. Woodenhead was reluctant to promote Ms. Awful-Nuisance.

What are we to think from this? That some other person told Ms. Woodenhead that Ms. Awful-Nuisance was a nincompoop? Did Ms. Awful-Nuisance call Ms. Woodenhead a nincompoop, or was it the other way around? Depending on what you're trying to say, one of the following would be clearer:

> Ms. Woodenhead had been told that Ms. Awful-Nuisance was a nincompoop, and so was reluctant to promote her.

> Since Ms. Awful-Nuisance had called Ms. Woodenhead a nincompoop, Ms. Woodenhead was reluctant to promote her.

Clarifying ambiguous references. Be sure you make it clear, at all times, who or what you're referring to.

> A large beam fell on me, pinning my head to the ground. This had to be removed before I could escape.

Yes, but did they get your head back on? Try this: "My head was pinned to the ground by a large beam, which had to be removed before I could escape." (This is a rare instance where the passive voice is clearer and more efficient than the active voice.)

> Although I was in it at the time, someone stole a suitcase out of my hotel room.

Must have been a large suitcase. Try, "Someone stole a suitcase out of my hotel room, although I was in the room at the time."

Avoiding subject-verb disagreement. The verb in a sentence must agree in number and person with its subject. This is a point on which it's easy to make mistakes.

> Every man, woman and child has to be rescued.

Here, many writers will make the mistake of using "have to be rescued," thinking that the verb must be plural to agree with all those men, women and children. But if you take the sentence apart, you'll find that the verb should agree with every man, every woman, every child. In other words, the singular "has" is better.

> Music, poetry and theatre are fine arts.

> The fine arts are things like music, poetry and theatre.

> The phrase "fine arts" means things like music, poetry and theatre.

In the first sentence, you have to use the third-person plural form of the verb—"are"—to agree with "music, poetry and theatre" which, together, are the subject.

In the second sentence, again, you use the third-person plural form, since the subject, "the fine arts," is plural.

But in the third sentence, the subject is singular, because the subject is, "The phrase 'fine arts.'" "Phrase" is singular, so you would use the singular form of the verb: "refers."

Avoiding structural inconsistencies. A sentence like, "Being handsome isn't as important as wealth" is awkward because you've constructed the parallel ideas differently from each other. "Being handsome" is a noun-adjective construction, while "wealth" is a simple noun. Far better would be, "Looks aren't as important as wealth," "Being handsome isn't as important as being rich," or "Being handsome isn't as important as being wealthy."

Frequently Misused Words and Expressions

CONSENSUS

Consensus means "general opinion," or "position acceptable to everyone involved":

> The consensus was that he wouldn't stay with the company much longer.

> Republicans and Democrats tried to reach
> a consensus on the bill.

Consensus does not mean "majority." And don't say "consensus of opinion."

DIFFERENT THAN

Different than is now so common that many people consider it standard. However, we must discourage this ugly construction. Use *different from!*

> A man's viewpoint is different from a woman's.

EKE OUT

Many writers mistakenly use the expression *eke out* to mean "barely achieve":

> The horse eked out a narrow victory.

> I eked out a tiny profit.

The standard definition of *eke out* is "supplement":

> I eked out my salary by winning at the racetrack.

> The Thanksgiving turkey was eked out
> by stuffing and mashed potatoes.

Eke is an old-fashioned word meaning "extra" or "more." The word "nickname" comes from the centuries-old expression "eke-name," which means "extra name."

EMPHASIZE

Most of us know that *emphasize* means "give special force or prominence to":

> She dressed to emphasize her figure.

> I emphasized the importance of speaking clearly.

However, some people think *emphasize* also means "feel what the other person is feeling." The word they want is *empathize:*

> I try to empathize with any customer who has a complaint.

ENORMITY

Enormity means "heinousness," or "dreadfulness." It does not mean "immense size."

> Because of the enormity of his offense, the judge
> sentenced him to death.

EQUALLY AS

If you want to sound really illiterate, just use *equally as*, as in:

> I'm equally as fond of Ms. Smith as I am of Ms. Jones.

As is implied in the word *equally*. In any case, in the above sentence, you shouldn't use *equally* at all. Just say, "I'm as fond..."

Use *equally* to precede a list to which it refers:

> I'm equally indebted to my boss, my assistant,
> my family and my dog.

EQUIVOCAL/EQUIVOCATE

Equivocal means "ambiguous," "questionable" or "misleading."

If you're *equivocating*, you're being deliberately vague or ambiguous in order to avoid committing yourself, or to mislead or confuse the person you're speaking with. *Equivocating* is not exactly lying; it's just not being entirely truthful.

Definition-wise, *equivocal* and *equivocate* do not have anything to do with words like "equal," "equivalent" or "equate."

IRREGARDLESS

Strictly speaking, it's not true that there is no such word as *irregardless*. Since so many people use it, we have to admit that it's a word. However, it's an illiterate word, and has no place in business writing. Use *regardless*.

LITERALLY

Many writers use *literally* when they mean *figuratively:*

> He literally stuck a knife in my heart and twisted it.

Really? Then why aren't you dead?

This is a very easy mistake to make. Many of us throw in the word *literally* as a "flavoring particle," just to make the sentence a little stronger—as you might say, "He's a total fool," instead of "He's a fool." Only use *literally* when you have to emphasize the fact that you really do mean something literally:

> After the burial, he literally danced on her grave.
> I was disgusted by this display of hatred.

MAJORITY

A *majority* means "more than half." It does not mean "the most." A *plu-*

rality means "more than any of the others, but not more than half." In other words, if Ms. Smith got 53 percent of the votes, she would have a *majority*. If she got 48 percent, Mr. Jones got 40 percent, and Ms. Brown got 12 percent, Ms. Smith would have a *plurality*, not a majority.

If more than half the people in a town were Catholic, then the Catholics would be in the *majority*. If the religious breakdown were 45 percent Catholic, 20 percent Protestant, 15 percent Jewish, 10 percent Buddhist, and 10 percent Muslim, then the Catholics would have a very large *plurality*, but not a majority.

Plurality also refers to the difference between one number and another. If the 435-member House of Representatives had 218 Republicans, 190 Democrats, 20 Communists, and seven Libertarians, then the Republicans would have a *majority* of one. (That is, 218 is one seat more than half of the total.) They would have a *plurality* of 28 over the Democrats.

MOMENTARILY

Momentarily means "for a moment," not "in a moment." If you say, "I'll be back *momentarily*," it means, "I'll be back, but only for a short time." If you mean to say that you won't be gone long, say, "I'll be back soon."

PARTY

Party can mean a group of people: "Mr. Jones and his party" means "Mr. Jones and the people he brought with him." A person can be a *party* to a contract, in a legal document, or *party* to a conspiracy. *Party* is not a synonym for "person." Don't say, "The party I spoke to yesterday," if you're referring to one person.

PENULTIMATE

Penultimate means "next-to-last." It does not mean "highest" or "greatest." Some people use phrases like, "This meeting is of *penultimate* importance," probably because penultimate is such an impressive-sounding word.

PRESENTLY

Presently means "soon" or "shortly thereafter."

> I'll be back presently.

> He lay on the floor sobbing for a while, but presently he composed himself.

Presently does not mean "now." "At present" does.

Commonly Confused Words

ACCEPT/EXCEPT

Accept means "take something that's offered":

> I proudly accept your nomination.

The noun—the act of accepting—is *acceptance*.

> I wrote my acceptance speech in three minutes.

Except, as a verb, means "exclude"; as a preposition, it means "excluding":

> I except my husband when I say, "All men are pigs."

> Nobody knows anything about good English,
> except George Orwell.

The noun *exception* can mean "the act of excepting" or "strong objection":

> I never forget a face, but in your case
> I'll make an exception.

> I take exception to our department being called
> "the personnel department."

ADVERSE/AVERSE

Adverse is related to the word *adversary* (opponent), and can mean "contrary," "unpleasant" or "disapproving":

> I had an adverse reaction to the medicine.

> He suffered many adverse circumstances.

> I was adverse to his suggestions.

Averse is related to *avert* (to move away from), and it means "likely to avoid." It almost always requires a preposition, usually "to."

> She's averse to talking about her marriage.

ADVICE/ADVISE

Advice is the noun; *advise* is the verb.

> I advised him to move to New York, and he took my advice.

ADVISE/INFORM

To *advise* is to give advice; to *inform* is to give information.

> I advised him to convert to Islam.

> He informed me that he was a Buddhist.

AFFECT/EFFECT

Affect has two meanings: To assume a mood or style in a contrived manner, or to have an effect (not an affect!) on something.

> He affected a pink carnation in his buttonhole.

> His constant drinking affected his performance at work.

Effect is a verb meaning "to cause," and a noun meaning "result." To have *an effect* on means "to cause a change in."

> Her innovations effected a dramatic rise in sales.

> The effect of his scolding was to make us all work harder.

> Her attitude had a positive effect on all of us.

AGGRAVATE/ANNOY

Aggravate means "make something worse."

> I aggravated my sprained ankle by running a marathon.

Annoy means "make angry or uncomfortable."

> That deodorant commercial really annoys me.

ALLUDE/ELUDE/ALLUSION/ILLUSION

To *allude* to something means to refer to it indirectly. Such an indirect reference is an *allusion*.

> She was alluding to my wife when she said,
> "I hope nobody's coming with you."

To *elude* someone is to slip away from him.

> My boss was going to ask me for that report, but I eluded her all day.

An *illusion* is something that appears real, but is not, or is much less impressive than it appears to be.

> China's military strength was an illusion.

> A magician's tricks are illusions.

AMORAL/IMMORAL

Amoral can mean "not related to morality" or "without morals."

> The question of what's good music and what isn't is an amoral issue.

> An amoral person has absolutely no sense of right and wrong.

Immoral means "morally wrong."

> An immoral person knows right from wrong, but misbehaves anyway.

ANXIOUS/EAGER

Anxious implies worry or fear; eager implies desire.

> I'm anxious about this exam.

> I'm eager to get it over with.

ANYMORE/ANY MORE

In modern American English, *anymore* means "nowadays."

> I don't get around much anymore.

Any more means "any additional."

> Is there any more beer?

AS/LIKE

Although *like* is commonly used as a conjunction in everyday speech (like it ought to be used, like some people might say), some people feel that *as* is more appropriate for formal speech and writing (as it's being used in this sentence, as your boss would probably prefer).

ASSURE/ENSURE/INSURE

You *assure* people (make them feel sure); you *ensure* something (make sure it will happen); you *insure* your life, home or health (by taking out a policy).

> I assured her that she wouldn't be fired.

> She ensured that he'd work late by promising him a bonus.

> I insured the package for $100,000.

BETWEEN/AMONG

Use *between* when referring to two or specific individuals. Use *among* when you're speaking of more than two or a group as a group.

> A long discussion took place between Tom and Dick. Harry wasn't there.

> A brawl broke out among the spectators.

BI/SEMI

Bimonthly means "every two months." *Semimonthly* means "twice each month."

BLOC/BLOCK

Block, of course, has many definitions. However, if you're talking about a group of people or organizations that has agreed to act as a unit, the word is *bloc*.

CAN/MAY

Can refers to capability, while *may* refers to possibility and to permission:

> I can touch the ceiling.

> I may propose to her tonight.

> You may jump out the window, if you like.

CAPITAL/CAPITOL

Capital has many meanings, while *capitol* has only one. *Capitol* refers to a building that houses a legislative body; in any other context, you'll use *capital*:

> The U.S. Capitol Building is in Washington, D.C., which is our nation's capital city.

> Each state also has a capital city, where you'll find the state capitol.

CENSOR/CENSURE

In its modern usage, to *censor* something is to suppress or exclude it to avoid giving offense or revealing sensitive information. Every time you stop yourself from cursing, or stop talking before you give away a secret, you're *censoring* yourself.

To *censure* someone is to scold him: In modern usage, it almost always refers to official, formal reprimands, as when the Senate votes to *censure* a member for misconduct.

COMPLIMENT/COMPLEMENT

A *compliment* is a phrase or gesture of courtesy, flattery or respect. *Complement* has many definitions, one of which is "to enhance or complete." Many people confuse these two words when referring to something that enhances or completes another thing. The following sentence uses both words properly:

> I complimented him on his red tie,
> which complemented his blue suit.

CONNOTE/DENOTE/IMPLY

Connote is similar to *imply;* it means, "to suggest something beyond the explicit meaning." The difference between *connote* and *imply* is that the speaker implies; his words connote:

> The term *nouveau riche* connotes ostentation
> and vulgarity, as well as wealth.

> By calling him a "smooth character," I implied
> that he wasn't altogether honest.

Denote means to stand for or refer to something explicitly:

> A black armband denotes the recent death
> of a friend or relative.

> The St. Andrew's Cross denotes Scotland.

CONTINUAL/CONTINUOUS

Continual means "done regularly." *Continuous* means "repeated or continued without interruption":

> His continual drug abuse affected his performance at work.

> The continuous drumming in the upstairs apartment
> kept me awake.

DEPRECATE/DEPRECIATE

Deprecate means "put down"; *depreciate* means "lose value":

> She deprecated her sister's taste in men.

> A new car depreciates by more than 50 percent
> as soon as you drive it off the lot.

DISCREET/DISCRETE

Both of these words are adjectives. *Discreet* means "prudent" or "tactful."

Discrete means "separate" or "distinct."

> He was too discreet to mention that
> she needed voice lessons.

> I write a regular column for the *Times*,
> but this essay is a discrete project.

DISINTERESTED/UNINTERESTED

Disinterested means "neutral," "unbiased," or "not influenced by personal considerations":

> We asked a disinterested person to settle our argument.

Uninterested means "not interested."

> My son is uninterested in his schoolwork.

ELICIT/ILLICIT

Elicit is a verb, meaning "to bring about." *Illicit* is an adjective, meaning "illegal" or "immoral."

> His firing elicited a strong protest from the rest of the staff.

> He was fired for illicit use of inside information.

EMIGRATE/IMMIGRATE

You *emigrate* from somewhere; you *immigrate* to somewhere. A person who does those things is an *emigrant* or an *immigrant*, depending on whether you're speaking of his departure or his arrival. To simply call someone an immigrant implies that he immigrated to the country you are in right now, or the country you were just now speaking of.

> I emigrated from Poland.

> I immigrated to the United States.

> He's an emigrant from Russia.

> My parents were immigrants.

EMINENT/IMMINENT

These two words have no relation to each other save for a similarity in sound and spelling. *Eminent* means "greatly respected"; *imminent* means "about to happen."

FARTHER/FURTHER

If something is *farther*, it's more distant:

> My house is farther from the office than yours.

Further refers to an extension of quantity, time or degree. In effect, it just means "more":

> Do you intend to investigate further?

In practice, the distinctions between *farther* and *further* have almost disappeared.

FLAUNT/FLOUT

To *flaunt* something means to display it ostentatiously (and often defiantly):

> She flaunted the jewelry her boyfriend bought her.

You *flout* a rule or law if you scornfully disobey it:

> He flouted the speed limit.

GOOD/WELL

In general, *good* is an adjective, used to modify a noun (He's a good worker). "*Well*" is an adverb, used to modify a verb (He played well). "I feel good" is standard English, as a way of indicating emotional well-being or physical vitality. "I feel well" means, "I do not feel ill." Otherwise, *good* is acceptable as an adverb only in informal expressions (I nailed him but good). You'll seldom use *good* as an adverb in business writing.

HISTORIC/HISTORICAL

Historic means "of importance to history." *Historical* means "a fact or occurrence of history," or "referring to history." Since the h in these words can be unstressed, many authorities prefer to speak of "an *historic* place," or "an *historical* fact"—even though they would say "a history of football." Other authorities feel that the use of "an" in this context is absurd. Whichever you choose—"an" or "a"—be consistent.

> July 4th is an (a) historic date.

> Your birthday is an (a) historical fact, but it is not historically important, so you can't call it an (a) historic event.

HOME/HONE

To *home in* on something means to seek out and attack something with great precision. (It refers to homing pigeons, which have extraordinary senses of direction.) Some writers mistakenly say *"hone in"*—possibly because *to hone* means to sharpen.

I/ME

No doubt you've heard plenty of people saying things like, "Just between you and I," or "He spoke to my wife and I." Using *"I"* where one should use *"me"* is a very common mistake—probably more common, in the business world, than using *"me"* instead of *"I."*

Some of us never recovered from the way our third-grade teachers gave us grief for using *"me"* incorrectly (as in "It's me," or "Him and me are going swimming."). These teachers did such a good job of curing us of our mistakes that many of us avoid using *"me"* in just about any situation. However, "He spoke to my wife and me" is perfectly all right, as you can tell by dividing the sentence in two: "He spoke to my wife. He spoke to me." Or try turning the sentence around: You would never say, "He spoke to I and my wife." On the other hand, many people do misuse the word "me." For instance, "It's me!" is substandard; "It's I!" is better, and you can see this when you state the sentence as "I am it!" "She's taller than me" is substandard. "She's taller than I" is better, because it would be just as proper to say, "She's taller than I am." But you wouldn't be likely to say, "She's taller than me am."

IMPLY/INFER

The speaker *implies*; the listener *infers*:

> He implied that he was thinking of quitting.

> I inferred from what he said that he didn't like his job.

INGENIOUS/INGENUOUS

Ingenious means "clever" or "resourceful."

> His method of making hats out of dried pumpkin shells is quite ingenious.

Ingenuous means "innocent" or "frank." (Disingenuous means "fake-innocent" or "hypocritical.")

> "That hairdo makes you look 20 years older," he said ingenuously.

> You're being disingenuous when you say,
> "Guns don't kill people; people kill people."

An easy way to remember the difference is by the sound of the words: *Ingenious* sounds like "genius"; *ingenuous* sounds like "genuine."

ITS/IT'S

"Its" is the possessive, meaning "belonging to it"—its claws, its beak, etc. You would think it would be spelled "it's" since most possessives are formed by adding 's (Jim's, the company's, etc.). But remember that the possessives of pronouns (his, hers, yours, its) are not formed with apostrophes! "*It's*" is the contraction for "it is" and for "it has," and its apostrophe represents the missing space and letters.

> Ah, English! It's a shame that it's got so many little tricks up its sleeve.

LAY/LIE

Lay requires a direct object; *lie* does not.

> I'm going to lie down.

> I want the tablecloth to lie flat.

> But:

> Lay down your arms!

The past tense of *lie* is lay:

> I lay down for a few minutes.

LESS/FEWER

In general, you should use *fewer* when you're referring to something that can be measured or counted, and *less* when you're referring to something that can't have an exact quantity placed on it.

> I have three fewer staffers than I had last year.

> I wear less clothing in hot weather.

In many cases, you'll use *fewer* to modify plural nouns even if there are no numbers involved:

> I saw fewer customers today than yesterday.

Use *less* to indicate diminishment:

There's a pint less in the bottle than there was an hour ago!

Less is also standard in many phrases involving distance, money and time:

I make less than $50,000 a year.

I did it in less than two hours.

It's less than a mile away.

LIGHTNING/LIGHTENING

Lightning is what you see in the sky. *Lightening* is what you do to your work load by making the intern do most of it!

MASTERFUL/MASTERLY

Masterly uses "master" in the sense of "master craftsman." It means "of a master"—in other words, "first-rate":

It was a masterly presentation!

Masterful uses "master" in the sense of "a dog and its master." It means "like a master"—in other words, "domineering":

He was masterful when the strikers confronted him.

NAUSEATED/NAUSEATING/NAUSEOUS

Nauseated means "disgusted" or "sick to one's stomach." *Nauseating* and *nauseous* both mean "causing nausea or revulsion." If you want to say that you're feeling queasy, use *nauseated*, not nauseous.

Her new perfume made me feel nauseated.

Her makeup job is nauseating, too.

Her entire appearance is nauseous.

ORAL/VERBAL

Oral means "spoken," as opposed to "written":

She gave me written instructions, and explained them orally.

Verbal means having to do with words or language. It can refer to spoken and written words.

He has a terrible temper, but he only expresses it verbally, never physically.

PERSECUTE/PROSECUTE

To *persecute* someone is to continually make trouble for him; to *prosecute* someone is to press civil or criminal charges against him.

> Hitler persecuted many ethnic and religious groups.

> You can't be prosecuted for making a face at someone.

PORE/POUR

To *pour* is to dump something out of a container. To *pore* over something is to read it very intently.

> If you like a book, you'll pore over it. If you don't like it, you might pour your tea onto it.

PRECEDE/PROCEED

Precede means "come before"; *proceed* means "go ahead."

> A precedes B in the alphabet.

> As soon as you've stopped screaming, we'll proceed with this meeting.

PREMIER/PREMIERE

Premier as an adjective means "most important." (Some people use it to mean "first in time," but this usage is almost extinct.) As a noun, it means "prime minister."
As a noun or a verb, *premiere* means the first performance or exhibit of a play, film or piece of music.

> The premier attended the premiere of my new play.

> The premier reason for doing it is that you'll be fired if you don't.

PRINCIPAL/PRINCIPLE

Principle is a noun, meaning a fundamental truth or law; *principal* is an adjective and a noun, and can mean the head of a school, a sum of money that accrues interest, or a person of the highest rank within a group.

> The principal of my school didn't have any principles!

> One of the principles of good chess is, "Watch the whole board."

> A principle of sound investment is to get a high interest rate for your principal.

He's a principal investor in the new bank.

He's the principal tenor in the opera company.

If you're referring to a person, you will always use *"principal"* rather than *"principle."* Just remember: The *principal* is your pal!

RIGHT/RITE

A *rite* is a ritual, procedure or ceremony. You'd speak of a "rite of passage," or the "rites of courtship." To spell the word differently wouldn't be right, even if it were *right!*

ROLE/ROLL

Role means a part or character in a play, or the function of an office:

He assumed the role of chairman while Mr. Baldwin was in the hospital.

A *roll*, among its other definitions, is a list:

You may search the roll of the saints, but you will never find one who smoked.

REGARDING/AS REGARDS/IN REGARD TO/ IN REGARDS TO/WITH REGARD TO

You can probably come up with another half-dozen variations. For business writing, though, the only one you need to know or use is *regarding*. The others say the same thing, only they use two or three words where one would do.

Regarding means the same thing as "about" or "concerning," and many people prefer to use either of those two words. However, *regarding* is acceptable:

Regarding yesterday's meeting: Was the boss right?

In very informal writing, you may abbreviate *regarding* as "re."

I have a question re your latest memo.

STATIONARY/STATIONERY

The paper you write on is *stationery*. If something won't move, it's *stationary*.

THAN/THEN

Than is a conjunction that helps form a comparative phrase:

> I have more black shoes than brown ones.

Then refers to a point in time or to a sequence of events:

> I was out of my mind then.

> "We shed bitter tears for our departed King,
> then we played bridge."

Then also joins with "if" to describe a fact contingent on one or more conditions:

> If it's a parrot, then it can talk.

However, sentences of this sort usually work just as well without using *then* at all.

THAT/WHICH/WHO

Many people believe that it's proper to use *that* in clauses that are essential to the meaning of the sentence and *which* in clauses that do not add to the meaning of the sentence:

> The tree that I planted last year is already six feet tall.

> His story, which he told in a trembling voice,
> was probably not true.

This distinction is dying out, however.

A thing is a *"that"* or a *"which,"* but a person is a *"who"*:

> From things that go bump in the night, good Lord, deliver us.

> People who wear dentures shouldn't take them out in public.

An animal can be *"that"* *"which"* or *"who,"* depending on whether or not you know the animal:

> A cat that was howling outside my window woke me up.

> My cat, who has a loud voice, wakes me every morning.

THEIR/THERE/THEY'RE

People who confuse these three words usually do so from carelessness, rather than from poor English skills. But in case you forget, here are the distinctions:

Their is a possessive, meaning "belonging to them."

There is a direction, meaning "at or in that place or point."

They're is the contraction of "they are."

> They're going there, to their house.

TO/TOO/TWO

This is another group of words that people often confuse due to carelessness: *To* is a preposition meaning, "in the direction of," as in, "I'm going to the store." It's part of an infinitive, as in "It's so easy to fall in love."

Too means "also," as in, "You come, too." It means "excessively," as in, "I'm too tired."

Two is the number.

TOE/TOW

It's easy to see why some people write *tow* the line instead of *toe* the line, when they mean "buckle down and work hard," or "be on your best behavior." *Toe the line* is correct, though. The term comes from an extinct rule of boxing: Years ago, at the start of a bout, both opponents had to stand with one *toe* touching a line drawn in the middle of the ring.

UNCONDITIONAL/UNEQUIVOCAL

Unconditional means "with no conditions attached," or "no matter what."

> The Germans surrendered unconditionally.

> He left me his entire estate, unconditionally.

Unequivocal means "absolutely clear, with no shading of meaning."

> I agree with you unequivocally.

> Her explanation was unequivocal.

WAIVE/WAVE

To *waive* something means to give it up, not to take advantage of it, or not to impose it:

> Since your payment was only a day late, I'll waive
> the penalty.

The suspect waived his right to remain silent.

A *waiver* is the act of waiving something or a written statement saying that you waive something.

WHO/WHOM

Whom is the prepositional case of who. That is, if it follows a preposition such as "for," "to" or "with," you should say whom:

With whom are we going?

To whom did you give it?

Technically, if you put the preposition at the end of the sentence, you should still say whom. However, who has become so common in this construction that, today, either of the following sentences would be considered standard:

Who did you give it to?

Whom did you give it to?

Do not use *whom* if there is no preposition: "Who shall I say called?" is standard; so is "Who did you punch?"

Spelling

If you're a poor speller, you're in good company. The novelist F. Scott Fitzgerald was notorious for his poor spelling. George Washington's and Andrew Jackson's letters are full of spelling mistakes, and they both ended up with their pictures on money! William Shakespeare would sometimes spell the same word two or three different ways on the same page.

English spelling is so irregular that it's almost impossible to come up with any rules to help you avoid mistakes. In some languages, like Spanish or Italian, each letter has a certain sound value and you can usually spell a word correctly just from hearing it. In English, if you hear the sound "sloo," you won't know whether to spell it "slough," "slue," or "slew," unless you know the context. On the other hand, if you see the word "slough," without a context, you won't know whether to pronounce it "sloo" or "sluf."

As you know, sometimes there are two or more "standard" ways of spelling (and pronouncing) a word. An ideal example is "misspelled." Both "misspelt" and "misspelled" are standard. You may use either one; just be sure you always use it, and not the other.

Probably every English-speaker in the world, if asked how to spell the color between black and white, would reply, "Either 'gray' or 'grey.'" And probably we've all spelled it both ways, sometimes on the same page!

About the only useful spelling rule that any of us remembers from school is "I before E, except after C." This rule means that if you're dealing with a word in which the letters I and E form the "ee" sound, the I will fall before the E, as in "field" or "grieve." But if the two letters come after a C, the E comes before the I, as in "receive" and "perceive."

Otherwise, good spelling is a matter of learning, practice and memory. To become a good speller:

• **Learn** by reading a lot.

• **Practice** by writing a lot.

• **Memorize** by looking words up in a dictionary and remembering how to spell them.

To remember how to spell a tough word, associate a funny phrase, and then a funny picture, with the word. For instance, you might look at the word "carburetor," and come up with "Car, berate her!" Now you have a picture of a car standing up on its rear wheels, scolding a woman. Think of this picture as you look at the correct spelling in the dictionary. When you next hear the word, and want to remember how to spell it, just think of the phrase and the picture. That will cause the printed word, spelled correctly, to pop into your head.

Another technique is to remember the context in which you first read the word. Take a mental photograph of the page where the word appears. If there are any graphics on the page, expecially photos or drawings, be sure to remember them. The more detailed the picture in your mind, the surer you'll be to remember the word.

Here are a few often-misspelled words. Note all the inconsistencies: For instance, if I'm *contemptIBLE*, why am I so *desirABLE?*

a lot (two words)

accidentally (two Cs, two Ls)

accommodate (two Cs, two Ms)

acquainted

all right (two words)

amateur (You'll often see the EUR ending in words we borrowed from French.)

appear (two Ps)

appropriate (two Ps)

carriage (two Rs, I and A)

character (What's that H doing there?)

commit (two Ms, one T)

commitment

committed (two Ts)

committed (two Ts)

committee (three double letters!)

connoisseur (two Ns, two Ses, and that French EUR ending)

conscience (Note the SCI representing the "sh" sound.)

conscientious

conscious

consensus (think of "consent")

contemptible (IBLE, not ABLE)

convenience

desirable (ABLE, not IBLE)

despair (pronounced "dispair" in informal speech, but spelled with an E) *defendant* (ANT, not ENT)

despondent (ENT, not ANT)

dispensable (ABLE, not IBLE)

divorce (The couple's paths diverted.)

embarrass (two Rs, two Ss)

fascinating (SC, not S alone)

finally (three syllables, two Ls)

fluoride (Remember that FLUOR prefix in words like "fluorescent"—the U comes before the O!)

foreign

forty (It should be "fourty," but it isn't!)

government (Remember the N.)

harass (one R, two Ses)

humorous (In British English, just to confuse us, it's "humourous.")

incidentally (five syllables, not four)

incidentally (five syllables, not four)*independent* (ENT, not ANT)

irresistible (IBLE, not ABLE)

laboratory (If you give a speech there, it's lab-oratory!)

liquefy (EFY, not IFY)

marriage (Two Rs married I and A.)

miniature (Minnie ate your dessert.)

necessary (One C, two Ses in the word.)

optimistic

permanent

rhythm (Remember where the Hs go.)

similar

sincerely (Remember the second E.)

Correcting Your Boss

Now that you know quite a lot about how to use the English language, it's likely that your boss will start to depend on your knowledge. He might, for instance, give you a very roughly written letter or memo and say, "Translate this into good English for me." Or he might just tell you, very generally, what he wants the letter or memo to say, and let you write it.

Let's deal with the former situation first. Say your boss has just given you the following letter, with orders to knock it into shape. Let's go over it and see what we can do:

Uglifruit Computer Corporation
1 East West St.
Requiem, Mass.
January 30, 1996

Mr. Theodore O'Shaughnessy
Ritter, Tod & Teufel Advertising
New York, NY

Dear Mr. O'Shaughnessey:

This is with regards to the communication I received from you on January 19. They were thoroughly gone over by my staff and I, and we made an all-out effort to thoroughly familiarize ourselves with the main points of your company's proposal. I emphasize with your need to know our decision as soon as possible, but, as I inferred in our previous conversations, we'll need to access more data before we can come to a final conclusion.

We just received the numbers on our most previous joint project, and I'm happy to tell you that with the help of your ad campaign we eked out a slight sales gain as against our major competitors.

Other good news...after being lost for some time in the dead files department, my secretary found a copy of the Adams report of which you had asked me to send you a copy. Since the demographics figures which are contained in it are especially apropo to the upcoming project, I suggest you go over the report which is enclosed with your marketing staff.

Also: Tell your creative people to please be sure to stress the advantages of our low-light Monitor in view of the fact that people that use computers that smoke are 3 times more likely to develop eyestrain.

Naturally, speed is of penultimate importance. We've got to be sure to role this product out before Giant Computer introduces something simular, as I understand they're working on. Let's keep both our ears glued to the ground to see what we can hear about their plans.

I should have a final answer for you by the end of this week, and we can set up a meeting sometime early next week.

Best Personal Regards,

T. Cordington Pendleton IV

To turn this perfectly awful letter into something readable, let's edit it twice: first for style, then for organization.

STYLE

Let's start with the inside address. Notice that Mr. O'Shaughnessy's name is spelled differently in the inside address and in the salutation. Find out the correct spelling of his name. Probably your boss has Mr.

O'Shaughnessy's card in his Rolodex; if not, you can call Ritter, Tod & Teufel and ask Mr. O'Shaughnessy's assistant.

Note also that your boss used the Post Office abbreviation for New York (NY) but the old-fashioned abbreviation for Massachusetts (Mass.). Except when you're addressing an envelope, the old-fashioned abbreviation is preferable.

First paragraph:
- The first sentence is better stated as "Thank you for your letter of the 19th." (If you're writing in response to a letter written in the same month, it's not necessary to mention the month in your letter.)
- "They were" in the next sentence should be "It was," since it refers to a letter.
- Use active voice ("My staff went over it") instead of passive ("It was gone over").
- It's "my staff and me," not "my staff and I."
- Avoid clichés such as "all-out effort."
- The word is "empathize." "Emphasize" means something else entirely.
- The listener infers, but the speaker implies.
- "...access more data" is business jargon. Avoid it.
- There's no such thing as a conclusion that isn't final!

Second paragraph:
- "Most previous" is awkward. Say "last."
- To "eke out" something means to add to it, supplement it, not to barely achieve it. "...as against" is gibberish. "...over our major competitors" is correct.

Third paragraph:
- An ellipsis (...) should almost never be used in a business letter. Here, a colon (:), followed by an initial capital, is correct.
- Who was lost in dead files? The report or the secretary?
- In any case, why tell the reader that you lose documents?
- Don't use the word "copy" twice in the same sentence.
- "...figures which are contained in it" is the passive voice. "...its figures" is shorter and clearer.

- The expression is "apropos." Use the English word: relevant.
- Is the report really enclosed with Mr. O'Shaughnessy's marketing staff?

Fourth paragraph:
- Use a comma, not a colon, after "Also."
- "Monitor" should not be capitalized.
- Spell out single-digit numbers.
- It's "people who" do so-and-so, not "people that." Use "that" only when talking about animals or inanimate objects.
- Is he talking about people who smoke, or computers that smoke?

Fifth paragraph:
- "Penultimate" means "next-to-last," not "vital."
- The second sentence contains two misspellings: "roll" and "similar" are correct.
- "...as I understand they're working on." should be "which I understand they're working on." Better yet, cut that phrase out: Why do you need it?
- The last sentence is a mangled cliché. If we keep both our ears glued to the ground, we won't be able to move. And we won't even mention "see what we can hear"!

Sixth paragraph:
- "Final" is a useless word in this context.
- If possible, propose a specific date for the upcoming meeting.
- "Personal" and "Regards" should not be capitalized.

ORGANIZATION

Just remember the One Big Rule:

Brevity, precision and clarity—and the greatest of these is clarity.

Some of the principles you should use to follow the One Big Rule are:

- Short sentences
- Active voice
- Plain words

- Lively style
- Correct spelling
- Consistent use of abbreviations

The following four rules will help you to write clearly:

- Never use a long word when a short one will do.

> Uglifruit Computer Corp.
> 1 East West St.
> Requiem, Mass.
> January 30, 1996
>
> Mr. Theodore O'Shaughnessy
> Ritter, Tod & Teufel Advertising
> New York, N.Y.
>
> Dear Mr. O'Shaughnessy:
>
> Thank you for your letter of the 19th. My staff and I have gone over your proposal. I'm sorry that I can't give you an immediate answer, but we're still waiting for other information to come in. I should have all the details for you by the end of this week.
>
> We just got the numbers on our last joint project. With the help of your ad campaign, we've made slight sales gains over our main competitors. Well done!
>
> I'm enclosing a copy of the Adams report, which you requested. Since its demographics figures are relevant to the upcoming project, I suggest you show it to your marketing staff.
>
> Also, ask your creative department to stress the advantages of our low-light monitor, especially the fact that it reduces eyestrain.
>
> Let's get together early next week. I understand Giant Computer is working on a similar product, and I want to get ours out ahead of theirs. (If you hear anything about what Giant is up to, please let me know right away!)
>
> Best personal regards,
>
>
> T. Cordington Pendleton IV

- If it is possible to cut a word out, always cut it out.
- Avoid the passive voice ("All vacations must be approved by the supervisor") when the active voice will do ("The supervisor must approve all vacations").
- Never use a foreign, scientific or jargon word if you can use an everyday English equivalent.

Ghostwriting

Suppose your boss calls you into his office and says, "The Men's Hatters Association of America has asked me to write a short instructional manual on how to buy a hat. It'll go out to all the hat stores in the country for customers to read, and it'll have my name on it, so I want it to make me sound intelligent, if you know what I mean."

At this point, you should stop your boss, and make him sit next to you at your computer as you take down everything he says.

Let him go on about what he considers to be the main points about buying hats. Any time you don't understand his meaning, stop him and ask for an explanation. Ask as many questions as you can think of to get him to elaborate. Ask him which points are more important than others.

When he's talked himself out, and you've recorded it on your computer screen or taken it down in shorthand, it's time to reorganize it all.

> **BOSS:** A lot of guys who wear hats, if they wear the same hat all the time, that becomes, like, a kind of trademark. Like you know that guy used to coach the Cowboys, Landry? He always wore that velour trilby. And Al Capone, he had that big wide white fedora. And Sherlock Holmes, and Senator Moynihan with that tweed thing he always wears.
>
> **YOU:** That's called a walker, I think. But what do they call that hat that Sherlock Holmes wore?
>
> **BOSS:** A deerstalker. And I'm sure you can think of a lot of other famous people you could identify by their hats.
>
> **YOU:** Winston Churchill, Malcolm X, Jean-Paul Sartre... .
>
> **BOSS:** Exactly. But here's the thing: Those guys all looked good in those hats because they fit their overall look. I mean, I see some guys, they think they're being real clever always wearing a San Francisco Giants cap no matter what else they're wearing, or a cowboy hat no matter whether they're wearing jeans or a tuxedo and like they think that's some kind of really cool trademark, but it's not, 'cause it's inappropriate. I mean, it's not always gonna be appropriate to wear the same hat all the time.

> Not to mention that these are the kind of guys, they're so
> proud of their hats, that they think they've gotta keep them
> on all the time. I want you to mention that, specially, if you're
> inside a building, you're supposed to take your hat off. Also, I
> might be old-fashioned, but I think you gotta take your hat off,
> too, if you're standing in the street talking to a woman. You
> meet a lady in the street, you take your hat off, and you keep
> it off as long as you're standing talking to her. You can put it
> back on if you and her start walking together, but not til then.

Start by putting everything he's said into complete sentences. For instance:

> Many men, if they wear the same hat all the time, turn the hat
> into something by which they can be identified. The former coach
> of the Dallas Cowboys, Tom Landry, always wore a velour trilby.
> Al Capone always wore a big wide white fedora. Sherlock Holmes
> always wore a deerstalker. Senator Daniel Patrick Moynihan always
> wears an Irish walker. Winston Churchill always wore a homburg.
> Malcolm X always wore a stingy-brim fedora. Jean-Paul Sartre
> always wore a beret.
>
> Those men all looked good in those hats because they chose
> hats that fit their overall look. Some men think they're being
> real clever if they always wear a San Francisco Giants cap no
> matter what else they're wearing, or always wear a cowboy hat
> whether they're wearing jeans or a tuxedo. They think that's
> a strong fashion statement, but it's not, simply because it's
> inappropriate to wear a hat without thinking about how it
> relates to the rest of your outfit.
>
> Some men are so proud of their hats that they keep them on
> all the time. If you're inside a building, you're supposed to take
> your hat off. It's also polite to take your hat off if you're stand-
> ing in the street talking to a lady. It's appropriate to put it back
> on if you and she start walking together, but if you're standing
> still, keep it off.

Now, this is still not very good writing, but at least you've put it into standard
English sentences. Having done that, you can cobble the raw material into stylish, lively prose—briefly, precisely and clearly, and especially clearly.

> If you've chosen your hat well and wear it consistently, it can
> become a way of identifying you. (Think of Daniel Patrick
> Moynihan's Irish walker; Sherlock Holmes' deerstalker; Winston
> Churchill's homburg; John Steed's bowler; Tom Landry's velour

trilby; Al Capone's wide, white fedora; Malcolm X's stingy-brim; Jean-Paul Sartre's beret.)

But don't make the mistake of gluing the hat to your head, so to speak. The above examples worked because each hat fit the wearer's overall costume. Men who wear the same hat every day, regardless of the rest of their attire, just look silly. A hat that's perfect with a business suit rarely looks right with jeans and a baseball jacket—and vice versa, God forbid!

Another common mistake is to almost never take your hat off, indoors or out. According to the laws of etiquette, you must remove your hat when you enter a building, or when stopping in the street to speak with a lady.

Your boss might look at this and say, "It's perfect." He might say, "This sentence sounds a little too formal," or, "I prefer the expression 'Heaven forfend' to 'God forbid.'" But his criticisms will probably be minor, and on the whole, he's likely to say, "You made me sound like a genius!"

Foreign Words and Phrases

In general, it's best to avoid using foreign words or phrases if you can find an English equivalent. In some cases, however, you will choose the foreign term—possibly because no English word expresses exactly what you want to say; possibly because you feel the foreign term will have more force.

But beware! Misusing a foreign term in business writing *really* makes you look bad! If you have the least doubt as to the spelling or meaning of a foreign term, look it up. If you can't look it up, don't use it.

Always write foreign words and phrases in italics unless they're so commonly used in English that they're considered English words. (For instance, you wouldn't italicize "caucus," which is an Iroquoian word that English-speakers adopted more than 200 years ago.) If the word is listed in a standard English dictionary, that means it's common enough to forgo italics.

Each entry on the list includes the phrase, the type of word or phrase it is, the language it comes from, pronunciation and definition.

(**n.**= noun; **v.**=verb; **adj.**=adjective; **adv.**=adverb; **exc.**=exclamation; **exp.**= expression; **con.**=conjunction; **prep.**=preposition; **Fr.**=French; **Gr.**=Greek; **It.**=Italian; **L.**=Latin; **Sp.**=Spanish; **Y.**=Yiddish)

ad hoc (adj., L., ad HOK): for a specific or temporary purpose

ad infinitum (adv., L., ad in-fin-ITE-um): forever; to the point of infinity

ad nauseam (adv., L., ad NOW-zay-am): to a sickening degree

àpropos (adj., Fr., ah pro-PO): relevant; timely; fitting

bête noire (n., Fr., bet NWAHR): person who brings trouble or bad luck

bona fide (adj., L., BO-na FEE-day): genuine

carte blanche (n., Fr., cart BLAWNSH): permission to do whatever it takes—legal or not

cause célèbre (n., Fr., cohz say-LEBRH): sensational controversy or legal case

c'est la guerre (exp., Fr., say la GEHR): that's war; such things happen in war; tough beans

c'est la vie (exp., Fr., say la VEE): that's life

chutzpah (n., Y., KHOOTS-pah): gall; nerve

coup d'état (n., Fr., coo day TAH): overthrow of a government, usually by force

coup de grâce (n., Fr., coo duh GRAHSS—note: Not coo day GRAH): killing blow

crème de la crème (n., Fr., KREM duh la KREM): best of the best

cum laude/magna cum laude/summa cum laude (adv., L., coom LOW-day; MAHG-na coom LOW-day; SOOM-ma coom LOW-day): with honor; with high honor; with highest honor

de facto (adj., L., day FAK-to): in effect, if not by law

déjà vu (n., Fr., DAY zha VOO): the idea that what is happening has happened before

de jure (adj., L., day YOO ray): determined by law

de rigeur (adj., Fr., duh ree GURR): required by unwritten law

éminence grise (n., Fr., ay-mee-NAWNSS GREEZ): the power behind the throne

enfant terrible (n., Fr., awn FAWN tay REEBL): person who stirs things up or behaves unconventionally

en masse (adv., Fr., awn MAHSS): as a large group

ergo (con., L., AIR-go): therefore

esprit de corps (n., Fr., es-PREE duh KOR): team spirit; team pride

eureka (exc., Gr., yoo-REE-ka): I've found it

ex post facto (adj., L., ex post FAK-to): concocted to punish an act that was legal when committed

fait accompli (n., Fr., FAY ta-com-PLEE): done deal

faux pas (n., Fr., fo PAH): social mistake

hoi polloi (n., Gr., HOY puh-LOY): ordinary people

in loco parentis (adv., L., in LO-co puh-REN-tis): in the role of a parent

in memoriam (adj., L., in meh-MO-ree-am): in memory of

in situ (adv., L., in SEE-too): in the original state

in toto (adj., L., in TO-to): in its entirety

je ne sais quoi (n., Fr., j'n say KWAH): that "certain something"

joie de vivre (n., Fr., ZHWAH duh VEEV): enjoyment of life

mea culpa (exc. or n., L., MAY-ah KOOL-pah): as an exclamation, "I am guilty"; as a noun, "confession."

mensch (n., Y., mensch): heroic person; good guy.

modus operandi (n., L., MO-dus o-per-AHN-dee): method of operation

noblesse oblige (exp., Fr., no-BLESS o-BLEEZH): noble (high-ranking) people must behave nobly

non compos mentis (adj., L., non KOM-pos MEN-tis): insane

nouveau riche (n., Fr., NOO-vo REESH): newly rich and ostentatious

persona non grata (n., L., per-SO-na nohn GRAH-ta): an unacceptable person

post-mortem (n., L., post MOR-tum): autopsy

prima donna (n., It., PREE-ma DOHN-na): demanding, self-important person

pro tempore (adj., L., pro TEM-po-ray): temporary

que sera sera (exp., Sp., kay seh-RAH seh-RAH); sometimes **che sarà, sarà** (It., kay sah-RAH sah-RAH): what will be, will be

quid pro quo (n., L., kwid pro kwo): tit for tat; something given in exchange for something

raîson d'être (n., Fr., RAY-zohn DET): reason for existing

savoir-faire (n., Fr., SAH-vwar FAIR): tact; suavity; grace under pressure

schlemiel (n., Y., shl'-MEEL): worthless, bungling person; loser

schlimazel (n., Y., shl'-MAH-z'l): luckless person

schmendrick (n., Y., SHMEN-drik): wimp

semper fidelis (exp., L., SEM-per fee-DAY-lis): always faithful

status quo (n., L., STAH-tus KWO): the existing order

terra firma (n., L., TEHR-ra FEER-ma): solid ground

tour de force (n., Fr., TOOR duh FORSS): extremely well-done task

vis-à-vis (prep., Fr., VEE zah VEE): towards

EXERCISES

Misused Words and Phrases

Some of these sentences contain misused words and phrases, and some don't. Find and correct the mistakes.

1. I had to run a mile further than I'd expected.

2. The Petersons invited me to they're house last night.

3. I shall be waiting for you next door.

4. A fly can't bird, but a bird can fly.

5. Dickens' novels had a profound affect on me.

6. It's I, not you, who's the real power behind the throne.

7. She presently has a thousand less votes than he has.

8. She went on and on about her grandchildren, and I became more and more disinterested.

9. Were you inferring by that remark that its foolish for us to try to form a union?

10. He smoked continuously, lighting one off the other, not even stopping momentarily.

Spelling

Find and correct the misspelled word in each of the following sets of five words:

1. aphid, aphorism, appathy, appetite, apprehend
2. charisma, chicanery, chihuaua, chimera, chromatic
3. emanate, emissary, emolient, emolument, emphasis
4. kimona, kiosk, kitchenware, kleptomaniac, knell
5. operative, opthalmology, optimistic, opinionated, oppress
6. socialist, soliloquy, soltitude, somersault, soothsayer
7. sophmore, sophistry, sorority, sorrel, southerly
8. veinous, veneer, venereal, ventral, ventrical

CHAPTER 5

Plugging in

Getting Started in Desktop Publishing

Desktop publishing software keeps on getting easier to use. Nowadays, it's routine for an assistant with no previous training to produce newsletters, reports, and other documents that used to require outsourcing. There are templates available on different software programs that allow you to do not only handsome newsletters and brochures but good-looking financial reports, including graphics.

Having the right software is only half the battle, however. You also have to understand how to lay out a page so that it is easy to read, attractive, and professional-looking.

There are plenty of books and courses available on desktop publishing that will teach basic page layout and optimal use of copy and graphics. But to get you started, here are some pointers:

FORMATTING TIPS

In producing manuscript copy, you can create near type-set quality documents by following a few word processing tips:

• Use only one space after periods, colons, exclamation points, and question marks. Because most computers have proportionally spaced fonts, you can get a more professional looking document than in the past from material produced on a typewriter.

• Use real quotation marks rather than "inch" marks. Use real apostrophes instead of "foot" marks as well. Most word processing programs have these. Check your computer handbook for instructions.

• Use em dashes. Typewriters use two hyphens to indicate a dash. The hyphen on a computer keyboard replaces the double hyphen with the typewriter. There should be no spacing on either side of the em dash.

• Use bold or italic type to highlight text. With the help of your computer, you needn't depend on underscoring anymore.

GRAB THE READER!

• Use big, bold banners in a distinctive type style, and quick, punchy headlines. Using numbers in headlines is especially effective ("Sales Go Up 15%"). When possible, use pictures with people in them.

• Use white space. A page that is packed chock-full is hard to read. Cut down the articles, or add a few pages, rather than crowd the pages you have. Leave a couple of lines of space between articles. Leave a line between the copy and a photograph or other graphic.

• While you don't want a dense-looking page, do fill up the page. If you're short on copy, lay it out loosely; never leave a gaping white hole at the end of the last column because you've run out of material.

• Don't overdo the graphics. A photo or two, or a piece of clip art, will make the page look livelier, but don't sacrifice content for the sake of artistry.

BE EASY ON THE EYES

• In general, serif type (a font in which the letters have little tails) is easier to read over long periods than sans-serif type (no tails, like this). However, sans-serif fonts tend to be more eye-catching. If you're going to use more than one type style in your publication, use sans-serif type for short articles (and for headlines) and serif type for longer ones.

• "Knock-out" type (white lettering on a dark background) is attractive but hard to read. Don't use it for more than a few words.

• To highlight short but important stories, put a tinted box around them. Don't use more than one or two boxes per page, though, and don't use a tint so dark that someone can't read the copy. (A 10 percent tint is usually about right.)

• Use "breakers." Breakers are anything that interrupts the flow of the text and forces the reader to pause for a second. The "bullets" used to mark each new point in this article are examples of breakers; so are the "subheads" that you see here. "Call-outs" (short, snappy quotes from a story, set in larger type) and "drop caps" (oversized capital letters set into the copy to indicate a new section) are also effective.

Breakers serve as "teasers," to keep the reader alert and interested; they're also mileposts, reminding the reader that she's finished another section of the story.

PROFESSIONAL SECRETS

• Probably the three most common layout mistakes are "bumping heads," "widows," and "rivers." Bumping heads occur when you start two stories side-by-side on the same page, so that the two headlines are right beside each other. Look at the front page of your morning newspaper, and you'll see that each article begins at a different level on the page, so that the eye can separate them easily. (A typical newspaper or newsletter front page has one headline at the extreme left, one at the extreme right, and a picture in the center, with a headline below it.)

A widow is a last line of a paragraph that contains only one word. If a widow occurs in the middle of the page, it's no problem. But when a story jumps from one column to the next, and the first line of the new column is mostly white space, it looks sloppy. The first line of a column should always run the full width.

Rivers are the opposite of bumping heads: A river occurs when two or more patches of white space appear side-by-side in adjacent columns. For instance, if you've got a widow in the middle of column one, next to the end of an article in column two, next to some white space above a graphic in column three, you've just cut the page in half.

• Nearly all word-processing and desktop publishing packages contain a spell-checking feature. These programs are not infallible. If the spell-checker says you're wrong, and you're sure you're right, check the dictionary.

Some software programs also have a grammar-check program. While you should develop your writing skills, and your organization may have a style book that disagrees with grammar-check, if you have access to grammar check on your computer, use it as a backup to your own editing.

• Develop a look, and keep it. You can identify each of your local papers at a glance by type styles, headlines, and standard ways of laying out the front page. Likewise, cover designs. If you maintain a certain look, people will immediately identify your publication and associate it with your company. If you're doing everything else right, that's what you want them to do!

GOING ONE STEP FURTHER

You may be asked not only to produce camera-ready pages but produce the report or brochure. That means you have to decide the kind of paper, grade and weight to use. Since specifying the right paper can significantly impact the final product, here are some tips from Creative Litho of Foster City, California:

Grades of paper. There are four grades:

Bond. This is the paper most frequently used for letterheads, business forms, and fast printing jobs.

Offset or uncoated book. Most commonly used for offset printing, this paper grade has a smooth, uncoated look.

Coated book. Great to use with bright colors, this glossy sheet provides excellent reproduction quality.

Text. Suitable for soft, gentle colors, this high-quality paper offers a nice texture.

Basic weight. Weight is used to distinguish papers. Coated papers are more compressed so when you go from uncoated sheets to coated, weight may have to increase to get the same thickness. This explains why paper specifications include both weight and grade.

"Basis weight" is the weight of 500 sheets of paper cut to a standard size. So, for instance, 500 sheets of 25 inches by 38 inches of 60# offset would weigh 60 pounds. The standard size for bond is 17 inches by 22 inches; for text, offset, and coated, 25 inches by 38 inches; and for cover stock, 20 inches by 26 inches. This may explain why two similar sheets of different grades may have different basis weights.

Looking at the grades and ranges of weight:

Bond. Usually 24# for stationery, 20# for copying, and 16# for forms.

Text. The most common weights are 70# and 80#, but weights range from 60# to 100#.

Offset. Most professional publishing houses use 50# to 70# stock.

Cover. This comes in 60#, 65#, 80#, or 100# weights.

What about recycled papers? Prices continue to be higher than virgin stock, but they are more widely available than in the past.

E-Mail

You will, without question, be communicating more and more by electronic mail (e-mail) in your office and outside. But there are suitable occasions for electronic transmittal and unsuitable ones. For instance, routine letters, memos and reports usually don't require electronic transmittal. Save e-mail for situations demanding urgent replies or communications.

Some situations shouldn't be the subject of e-mail, either. For instance, personnel problems should be handled in face-to-face meetings, not through electronic communications. Nor should you respond to a negative e-mail message when you are still angry or upset about the message.

When you use e-mail, proofread your document carefully.

Unfortunately, many writers, when they start using e-mail, get into the habit of writing very informal, sloppy, downright illiterate letters—as if the difference between regular mail and e-mail were the same as the difference between a formal dinner and a meal consumed while standing in front of the refrigerator.

This can't be permitted. Whether you're writing a letter on paper or online, a letter is a letter—and a business communication is a business communication. There is no excuse for not following the same rules of grammar, spelling, usage, format, and protocol when writing e-mail as you would follow when writing a non-electronic letter or memo.

The only exception has to do with formatting: Naturally, it's impossible to send e-mail on your company's letterhead, and in most cases, it's impossible to use certain formatting techniques such as paragraph indentation or typing copy any way other than flush left.

Other than that, you must behave just as though you were using an old-fashioned manual typewriter. That means complete, formal letters and memos in good English.

To avoid sloppy habits, don't compose e-mail using your server's facilities. Instead, if you can, compose your e-mail on your word-processing program, edit and proofread it thoroughly, then transfer the text to an e-mail file.

Do not use any of those cute little symbols that have become fashionable in online chat rooms, such as :) or @-> ->. They are okay for personal communications, but they have no place in business.

When sending e-mail, stick to short paragraphs. E-mail wasn't intended for long documents, and you should discourage its use for these. But increasingly managers are using e-mail to send long proposals or reports to speed delivery. So there may be occasions when you will be working with a multi-screen document. When that is so, use an executive summary on the first screen.

Clearly state on the subject line your topic in 25-30 characters. If necessary, use the subject line to tell recipients how to follow up. For instance, "Distribute Quarterly Report" makes a better subject line than "Quarterly Report." Some people get as many as 100 e-mail messages a day, and a well-written subject line will help them in selecting those messages to read first.

Ellipses have no place in any business communication. That includes e-mail. Avoid excessive use of dashes and slashes as well. They can make your message confusing. Similarly, avoid overusing exclamation marks. Use of all capitals suggests you are yelling at the recipient. Don't use them. Use upper and lower case letters as you would in any business communication.

One final tip on writing e-mail messages: E-mail allows a message to be received, read, commented on, then the message with comments forwarded to another. You end up with a long chain of comments. When you receive such a message, paraphrase the initial message and subsequent comments and respond rather than perpetuate the chain. It makes for easier reading.

CHAPTER 6

Answers to Exercises

Terminology

I. 1. My (possessive pronoun) cat (noun) is (verb) completely (adverb) black (adjective).

2. Everything (indefinite pronoun) that (relative pronoun) I (personal pronoun) say (verb) is (verb) a (indefinite article) lie (noun).

3. I (personal pronoun) work (verb) for (preposition) a (indefinite article) company (noun) called (adjective) Dobrian, Logart & Frances (proper noun—functioning here almost as an adverb!).

4. What (interrogative pronoun) are (verb) you (personal pronoun) talking (verb) about (preposition)?

II. 1. My cat (subject) is completely black (predicate).

2. Everything that I say (subject) is a lie (predicate).

3. I (subject) work for a company called Dobrian, Logart & Frances (predicate).

4. I threw you a curve with "What are you talking about?" It's actually a compound sentence, with several words that are simply implied, not written. Including the implied words, the sentence would read, "What is it that you are talking about?"

In this sentence, "What" is the subject of the first clause; "is it" is the predicate. "That" is a conjunction that joins the two clauses. "You" is the subject of the second clause; "are talking about" is the predicate.

Punctuation

I. 1. **I've had some tough times in the past two years, but that was the toughest day of my life.**

   A comma separates the two clauses in the sentence.

   2. **On the Senate floor, one of the Republican party's major bills is in trouble. The Democrats on the Appropriations Committee, which must approve it, seem intent on talking the bill to death.**

   Put a comma between the two clauses in the first sentence, and on both sides of the explanatory phrase, "which must approve it." If you wish to draw a closer relationship between the two sentences, you may use a colon, instead of a period, after the word "trouble."

   3. **We're talking about the right to know: making sure people have access to the information they want in a timely manner and in a form they can understand.**

   A colon and a period are all the punctuation you need here. Since the material that follows the colon is not a complete sentence, do not capitalize "making."

   4. **Although it was thought to be broadly accurate, Bede's history was written almost 300 years after the events it describes—which is rather like us writing a history of Elizabethan England based on hearsay.**

   The dash here sets off the final clause more distinctly than a comma would have done.

   5. **Oddly, McCormick never called for two of the most common shortenings: *tho* and *thru*. He just didn't like them—which, of course, is all the reason that is necessary when it's your newspaper!**

   Use a comma after "Oddly" to indicate that the word modifies the entire sentence. The dash isolates the editorial remark (although a comma would have been acceptable), and the exclamation point acts as a sort of written laugh track. (If you'd wanted to de-emphasize your own joke, you could have used a period instead.)

   6. **Webster's first work, *A Grammatical Institute of the English Language*—consisting of three books: a grammar, a reader**

and a speller—appeared between 1783 and 1785, but he didn't capture the public's attention until the publication in 1788 of *The American Spelling Book.*

You could have used parentheses instead of dashes. The colon in the parenthetical phrase introduces a list. You could, if you wished, have placed commas around the phrase, "in 1788," but that might make the sentence even heavier-looking than it is!

7. Outside the New College chapel, Spooner rebuked a student by saying, "I thought you read the lesson badly today." "But, Sir, I didn't read the lesson!" protested the student. "Ah!" said Spooner, "I thought you didn't!"

This passage has three exclamation points, indicating, respectively, a strong protest, an interjection, and a punch line. Note that in the first two cases, the exclamation point takes the place of a comma. And did you get all the quotation marks in the right places?

II. Some of the following sentences could be punctuated better, and some are acceptable as they are. Find and correct the mistakes:

1. Before the Windsors' honeymoon was half over, the Devil, in the plausible guise of Charles Bedaux, had devised a sorry piece of work for the brother whom George VI had unwisely left in idleness.

This is acceptable as it stands.

2. The Duke did not care for Maxim's and the Tour d'Argent: They were the most celebrated restaurants but also the most expensive.

Since the second clause is rather long and complicated, it's better to substitute a colon for the semicolon, leave two spaces, and capitalize "they."

3. Reporters, temperamentally and traditionally, are skeptical—and perhaps justifiably so—whenever the personal honesty of a public official is questioned.

The commas serve to clarify the first clause. The dashes set off the writer's side comment. Parentheses also would have been acceptable.

4. At 6:45 (still 15 minutes before poll-closing time in the West) Eric Sevareid of CBS reported, "We are pretty confident now

of a Kennedy victory: All of the computing machines are now saying Kennedy."

That semicolon that introduced the quote was obviously a typo. Use a full colon to separate the two clauses in the quote, and capitalize "All," since that clause can stand as a complete sentence.

5. **If you're watching a black-and-white movie, it's actually better to have a black-and-white television.**

Without hyphens, this sentence is unclear: You might be talking about watching a movie about black and white people on a television that's painted black and white.

6. **"Do you think he's innocent?" the lawyer asked.**

Include the question mark within the quote.

7. **In the entire history of the case, both before the Committee on Un-American Activities and in Hiss's two trials for perjury, no one could be found who could remember George Crosley—except Patricia Hiss.**

This is acceptable as it stands.

Plurals, Possessives, Abbreviations, Capitalizations

1. **I'll be arriving on Friday, Aug. 18, 1995.**

Days of the week shouldn't be abbreviated; August may be, but it needs a period.

2. **"Keeping up with the Joneses" is an old expression.**

The plural of "Jones" is "Joneses," without an apostrophe.

3. **President Bush was once the head of the C.I.A.**

Don't start a sentence with an abbreviation.

4. **Woodrow Wilson was the only President of the United States to have a Ph.D.**

"Ph." abbreviates one word. You need not use the word "degree," since, in modern usage, it is implied in abbreviations for doctoral degrees such as Ph.D., M.D., D.V.M., and D.D. In any case, the word should not have been capitalized.

5. **Phenomena such as comets and eclipses happen rarely.**
   The singular is "phenomenon"; the plural is "phenomena."

6. **One of my favorite reference books is the *Reader's Encyclopedia*.**
   Titles of books should appear in italics. (You may underline them, if you're using a typewriter.)

7. **I was praying with my brethren from the Universal Life Church.**
   "Brethren" is an acceptable alternative plural form of "brother," especially in a figurative sense, but it should not be capitalized unless it is part of the name of an organization.

8. **Mick Jagger is the Rolling Stones' most famous member.**
   This sentence is acceptable as it stands.

9. **Many Americans love comedy shows from overseas, such as *Monty Python's Flying Circus*.**
   "Americans" should be capitalized.

10. **I spoke for several hours with Professor Einstein, who explained that his theory of relativity was just a wild guess.**
    "Theory of relativity" is not a proper name, and should not be capitalized.

11. **A Muslim may have as many as four wives.**
    This sentence is acceptable as it stands.

Numbers

Thirty-six thousand, six hundred sixteen.

Four hundred six.

Twenty-six point six-five, or twenty-six and sixty-five hundredths.

Six and seven-eighths.

One million, eighty-six thousand, nine hundred twenty-four-and-a-half, or one million, eighty-six thousand, nine hundred twenty-four point five.

Proofreading

I. Muhammad Ali regained the Heavyweight Championship by defeat- *b.b*
ating George Foreman in 1974. He lost the title to Leon Spinks in
1978 and regained it later that year. Following his rematch with
Spinks, he hinted that he was retiring. Over the next two years, the
WBA and the WBC recognized different claimants as Ali's successor.
In 1980, Ali "unretired" and made a comeback against the WBC
claimant, Larry Holmes. Since the claim to the title was in dispute at
that time, And since Ali had not lost his title int he ring, he must be
regarded as having been the defending champion—and Holmes, the
challenger, in that fight.

Thus, intellectually honest historians generally agree that Holmes won
the Heavyweight Championship by defeating Ali in nineteen-eighty.
Since then, that title has changed hands in the following succession:
Michael Spinks, Mike Tyson, James Douglas, Evander Holyfield,
Riddick Bowe, Evander Holyfield, Michael Moorer, George Foreman.
In each case, the title changed hands in the ring; in no case was an
elimination tournament involved.

While You might be right that the officials gave a bad decision
in the Foreman-Schultz fight (and even that point is nowhere near
so black-and-white as you'd have us believe), to argue that Forman
has no legitimate claim to the title is simply pernicious.

II. As you see from this list of ingredients, chef Jacques Pépin makes
chocolate cake with almost no flour:

> *12 ozs. semi-sweet chocolate*
> *11/2 sticks sweet butter, softened*

8 large eggs

1 cup sugar

1 teaspoon grated orange rind

2 cups almonds ground in the blender (yields 2 1/4 cups ground)

1/2 cup fresh breadcrumbs (about one slice bread)

1 cup heavy cream, whipped

Fog Index

I.   104 / four sentences = 26

26 + nine long words = 35

35 / 10 = 3.5

3.5 x 4 = 14

Press Releases

Here's one way to make the release more useful to the reader. (And did you notice that the phone number in the body copy was different from the number at the top of the page?)

PRESS RELEASE

Contact: William Gladstone (212) 779-8826

METS HAVE NEW NAME, NEW OWNER

NEW YORK CITY, March 1, 1996—Joseph Dobrian, a freelance writer based in Manhattan, bought the New York Mets baseball club this morning for $80 million.

Dobrian said he will change the team name to The Moderates, release all Met players from their contracts, and hire all new players.

"I'm also going to build a new baseball park, probably near Wall St.," Dobrian revealed. "I'm going to move the Mets out of Shea Stadium as soon as I can.

"Eighty million dollars was a small price to pay. I raised the money in just a few days by selling some of my poems. The Moderates will win the pennant this year, and four years out of every five hereafter, indefinitely."

For more information, contact William Gladstone at (212) 779-8826.

Misused Words

1. I had to run a mile **farther** than I'd expected.

2. The Petersons invited me to **their** house last night.

3. I shall be waiting for you next door. (No mistakes.)

5. Dickens' novels had a profound **effect** on me.

6. It's **I,** not you, who's the real power behind the throne. (This is acceptable. You wouldn't say "It's **I,** not you, who am..." The verb "to be" has to correspond to the pronoun **"It,"** not to **"I."**

7. She **currently** has a thousand **fewer** votes than he has.

8. She went on and on about her grandchildren, and I became more and more **uninterested.** (You could just as well have said, "...less and less interested.")

9. Were you **implying** by that remark that **it's** foolish for us to try to form a union?

10. He smoked continuously, lighting one off the other, not even stopping momentarily. (No mistakes.)

Spelling

The standard spellings of the misspelled words are:

apathy

chihuahua

emollient

kimono

ophthalmology

solitude

sophomore

ventricle

Index

The Take-Charge Assistant

Business Writing Skills

by J. Dobrian

Stock #6410/$14.95/$13.45 AMA Members
plus shipping & handling

All essentials of good writing are covered...

*Punctuation
*Grammar
*Use of foreign terms
*How to write effective letters,
  memos, reports, job descriptions,
  press releases, and resumes.

Also covered in **Business Writing Skills** are
**writing to your audience, editing and proofreading,
do's and don'ts from the experts, ghost-writing, getting
started in desktop publishing, e-mail, and other helpful topics.**
Each chapter contains exercises to help you build confidence
and assess your progress toward improved writing.

For Multiple Copy
Discount Information,

CALL

℃ 1-800-262-9699/1-518-891-1500 (Outside the U.S.)

Attention Office Professionals!

Treat Yourself to Something GOOD... for a Job Well Done!

Treat yourself to a Charter Subscription to **The Take-Charge Assistant,** AMA's monthly newsletter that will help you sharpen your professional skills and provide you with greater problem-solving capabilities in a changing work environment.

Monthly Departments include...

*Figures and Finance
*Writer's Lab
*Helpful Checklists
*"What Would You Do" Case Studies
*Your Personal Management
*Career Counsel

A Charter Subscription includes...

*12 monthly issues
*Yearly subject index for easy reference
*Preferential notification of all products and services AMA provides for secretaries and administrative assistants

The Charter Subscription rate is $75 per year/$67.50 for AMA Members. Call our Toll-Free Hotline to order with any major credit card and receive an EXTRA TWO ISSUES FREE—it's our way of saying 'thank you' for not having to bill you. Or we can bill you or your organization.

CALL TOLL-FREE TODAY!
© AMA HOTLINE:
(800)262-9699.
Outside the US, call (518)891-1500.
Fax: (518)891-0368

The Complete Job-Finding Guide for Secretaries & Administrative Support Staff
By Paul Falcone

High-paying executive secretarial jobs are one of the fastest-growing career categories out there. Yet finding—and landing—one of these plum jobs is impossible without a solid strategy and a little help from the experts.

This insightful guide shares the secrets of corporate America's highest paid administrative assistants and executive secretaries. It provides readers with:

- **Sophisticated tools and strategies for résumé writing, interview preparation and follow-up**

- **A way to handle tough situations, and avoid hot buttons**

- **An understanding of vital employer research methods**

- **An insider's view of the hiring process: what employers value and need, how these are changing, and how job-seekers can meet these needs.**

PAUL FALCONE *(Valencia, CA) has extensive experience as a manager, recruiter, and director of training, staffing, and human resources development. He has published numerous articles on employment-related topics.*

Career
Paperback • $16.95/AMA Members $15.25
Stock# 07885

Administrative Assistant's & Secretary's Handbook
J. Stroman and K. Wilson, edited by Susan Heyboer O'Keefe

A truly outstanding secretary or administrative assistant is a rare find. This comprehensive but compact guide sets the standard for any secretary or administrative assistant who wants to be perceived as a skilled professional.

The essence of a good assistant is efficiency and versatility, and this guide sets forth *all the skills* a reader needs, including a detailed section on the use of computers. Topics include:

- **Daily duties • Telephone usage (standard, conference calls, international)**
- **Travel arrangements • Record-keeping • Basics of computer hardware**
- **Overview of word processing, databases, spreadsheets, and communications**
- **Business and legal documents (form, appearance, and content)**
- **English grammar, punctuation, and usage • Bookkeeping and banking**
- **Hints on international trade • A glossary • and much more!**

JAMES STROMAN *is a professional secretary who has served a wide range of individuals, including an army general, a governor, numerous executives, and the owner of a football team.* KEVIN WILSON *is a certified quality professional and heads up several companies.* SUSAN HEYBOER O'KEEFE *is the editor of a major secretarial newsletter.*

Career
Hardcover • $22.95/AMA Members $20.65
Stock# 00273

AMERICAN MANAGEMENT ASSOCIATION

Publisher of:

Compensation & Benefits Review

HRFocus

Management Review

Organizational Dynamics

Supervisory Management

The President

The Take-Charge Assistant

AMA also sponsors the:

AMA Conference and Exposition
for Executive Secretaries & Administrative Assistants

For more information, call:
800-262-9699
Outside the US, call (518) 891-1500